# DRAW A HEART AROUND IT

# DRAW A HEART AROUND IT

A Revolutionary Mental Health Treatment
for Individuals and Companies

Cindy Willcocks

Printed in the United States of America

First Printing, 2019

ISBN 13: 978-1-9160745-0-7

# Contents

# Acknowledgements

I FEEL AN OVERWHELMING SENSE of achievement in taking a simple idea about sharing a message to a wider audience and creating a readable model for everyone. Writing a book is rarely a solo endeavour and I have such high regard, appreciation and love for the people who have enabled me to bring this book to life. Thank you from the bottom of my heart for encouraging and helping me to bring the L.OV.E Leadership model to the world.

Thank you to Zoe Marie Vigus for her honesty and reveal of her own life experiences. I hope this openness will inspire others reading her story to go on and achieve incredible things with their lives, just as Zoe has done.

I am filled with gratitude towards everyone who has contributed to the book: The 'Wellness Warriors' who answered questions and shared personal accounts and professional reflections to assist me in conveying the model of L.O.V.E Leadership to a broad audience—Kirsten Davenport, Helen Davies, Dr. Gill Green, Diana Guy, Wendy Hannon, Clint Jones, Jane Mitchell, and Gina and David Smallridge—my daughter, Laurie Willcocks, and sister, Lucy Willcocks. I also want to acknowledge the bravery of the courageous contributors who have chosen to remain anonymous.

Special thanks to Candi S. Cross and her business You Talk I Write who I thoughtfully selected to assist and guide me to achieve the end result. Candi has been my confidante through the entire process, showing compassion and patience and using her magical flair to help me to create a powerful totem.

There are so many people to thank, including my many supporters, friends and family members, including my stepchildren and grandchildren, who have all shared moments with me that have shaped my story. Especially to my daughter, who has filled my life with a desire to change the world one step at a time to create a place that I want her and others to be able to live and thrive in; Laurie is my world and knows it!

My final message is to my husband, who has given me room to breathe and repair, and the encouragement to show my colourful butterfly wings to the world. We have grown together to find the true meaning of love and respect with a tenderness that I have not always known. Andy is my soul mate, who I love for what he is and for what I am when I am with him. He loves me for who I am, as I do him, which has meant we have given each other room to be individuals as well as a strong partnership, achieving many things together. I'm looking forward to the next steps on our journey.

# Preface

I WAS BORN IN 1976, the eldest of three children to working-class parents. Brought up on a council estate in Plymouth, Devon, England, it was here that I learned to develop the survival skills to take me through life's pleasures and pains.

In my parents' search for a better life for me, leaving my comfortable roots led me to a secondary education, which I didn't quite fit into. As a result, I left school with low self-esteem and low self-confidence, as well as my six GCSEs graded A-C, which the educators had doubted my ability to achieve. I have continued to be underestimated at times throughout my adult years, too, which I have learned to overcome and depersonalise; this has served me well in life.

The greatest impact on my life was the birth of my daughter. Her presence and my love for that has educated me in ways beyond anything else. Alongside her arrival, I was widening my horizons and developing aspirations during my training as a Registered Mental Health Nurse, which I had accidently fallen into. There have been people who have had a positive effect during my life, and it's what I've done with my experiences rather than what they have been, which has shaped me. My passion for helping others has been a continuing motivator for me to offer guidance and support to them.

The consolidation of life's experience and travelling my own journey to self-actualisation enabled me to package the L.O.V.E

Leadership model to share with all of you. I am so excited that you are reading this book and wish you a complete journey to be the best version of you and encouragement to love exactly who you are. Each stage will encourage you to focus and overcome any obstacles you may experience just as it did for me.

How you conduct yourself as a leader will shape your future and I hope that of others, so I wish you every happiness in your search to love yourself and achieve your goals.

Warm wishes,
*Cindy Willcocks*

# Foreword

**A** PERSON WITH A BROKEN leg isn't defined by their health, nor should a person with mental illness.

Stigma is recognised as having a profound effect on the lives of people, perhaps even leaving people being viewed unfavourably and as the world continues to try and address the stigma associated with the *mental health* term, there remains so much work and progress to achieve in this area.

Cindy's work to promote a 'Mental Health 5 a Day' campaign in partnership with children and young people, as part of an early implementer site in 2009, formed a UK national agenda for the National CAMHS Support Service (NCSS), "Tackling the Stigma Associated with Mental Health" (Warner-Gale, 2011). The work received further national coverage in the UK, presented by Cindy at the 2009 annual conference for The National Association of Primary Mental Health Work and CAMHS Training, in Newcastle. The blueprint had a positive impact in reducing stigma; the campaign is still used in health practice today.

*The American Journal of Public Health* featured an article by Pescosolido et al (2013), acknowledging that small-scale efforts of individuals to tackle the stigma will continue to be challenged by the reinforcement from the larger culture. Fear and ignorance about mental illness contributes to discrimination, eroding self-confidence, making it more likely for people to withdraw from society and create barriers to accessing healthcare.

Everyone has mental health and it's important to practice maintaining good mental health; the mental health of populations will only improve through coordinated and sustained efforts to promote such.

I recall my past experiences where there was so much stigma surrounding mental health, alongside a reticence to even acknowledge *mental health.* As a society, we are moving towards acceptance that as human beings, we all have mental health—making things a little easier to talk about openly.

I feel that my experience of mental illness stripped me of my confidence completely. I went from being someone who would perform in front of hundreds of people, to wanting to do nothing except sit in a dark room with the covers over my head. I hated the sun coming up and daylight. I was someone who previously loved life but now dreaded every day. It wasn't until after I recovered and talked to others, that I realised how many people have experienced and continue to experience the suffering.

When I look back on my illness in medical notes and psychological reports, it feels like I'm reading about someone else. *Not me.* I have flashbacks to concerned conversations I overheard my mother and sisters engrossed in with professionals. They were begging those professionals to help me. I remember my mother and I waiting in my local doctor's office when I felt completely lost. At that time, it seemed that general practitioners had a limited understanding about mental health problems and illness and responded by prescribing the same medication to everyone, regardless of their mental health issue, leaving me to question whether they would give the same medication to someone with a broken leg as a tummy pain.

My specific problem was referred to as 'severe responsibility obsessive compulsive disorder' and my family had pushed for me to be seen. The doctor said that I would probably be seen by a consultant in something like seventy-two days. I remember my mother responding to the doctor and saying, "She might not make seventy-two days!" As reported by the media, long waits for help remain a pressure faced within our current integrated Health and Social Care systems.

Due to my experience, I often wonder about people suffering alone without a supportive family or friend to fight for them. How are they heard? And who promotes their voice? Advocating for what you need isn't easy when you are not feeling well. Believe me, I know! That is what connected me with Cindy.

Cindy's ethos of spreading unconditional love and L.O.V.E Leadership, in particular, empowering others and supporting people to have a voice, makes such a difference. For that reason, I want this book to reach the masses. The need for change is there in everyday life. How many people do we see sleeping on the streets, often as a result of mental illness, or because they have lost feeling of any control of their own minds yet we walk on past them? We can't be sure of their story and what we do know is that they are people just like us. They are people who have often lost their identity, their voice, their jobs, their homes, their network of support—friends and family—their hopes and dreams. They are people who need a voice, just as we all do. Through the focused areas of L.O.V.E Leadership, people will begin to see things differently, things they hadn't noticed before, enabling them to take action to build the future they want to be in.

I've found Cindy to be a dynamic person with a presence that makes everyone feel included and like they matter. Whether it is an individual or a company receiving this book, I hope it reaches people that need it the most, the people who have come to accept being ignored but deserve to be heard, and people who may not even be aware of the struggles they may face. Everyone, as Cindy says, deserves to be heard and be the best version of themselves they can be. Everyone needs L.O.V.E.

*—Zoe Marie Vigus, Acting, Speech and Confidence Coach*
*Former PA to Film Director Michael Winner*

# Introduction

## *Everyone Has Mental Health*

"How do you feel?" is the first question you hear when you go the doctor's office or chat with a friend after being confined for days in your comfy clothes with a really bad cold or the flu. You may have never thought about the moment when you actually get to describe how you feel to an attentive ear. However, for anyone who has had the experience, it's pretty gratifying and comforting. Although, how easy is it to respond to the question asked in a truthful way rather than automatically responding with the expected 'fine'? (To me, 'fine' reminds me of my time spent as drugs worker and manager, where the well-known acronym was used by people working and receiving treatment in a detox service for addiction, which actually meant the complete opposite to being fine. If you want to know what it stands for you'll have to contact me!)

If you think about this talking point more deeply, when was the last time your manager, colleague, tutor or neighbour, or anyone else you see regularly, genuinely asked you that simple yet mighty question and wanted your honest response? In fact, when did you ask anyone the same question and wait for their honest response? Your response may differ when thinking about your personal and professional life, or it may not; it's something that I encourage people to reflect upon.

As a hard-working, grinding society, we've been led to believe that this question should only be employed toward a physical affliction—an ailment that is seen, easy to detect, and even easier to treat. Otherwise, the perceived risk is opening a gigantic can of worms, making things worse for the individual, as mental health is just *too overwhelming* to address. After all, things need to get done. Businesses need to run. Money needs to be made. Supply chains of information, products and services operate nonstop. You likely play a role in at least one of them.

These days, despite your talent, brains, heart, charisma, you may rarely be asked how you feel, especially if it is known that everything may not be okay in your world. People can become avoidant of situations or discussions. Some people worry about the impact of their questioning upon others, as they fear the answers they may get and perhaps not know what to do with those answers. Other pressures to avoid such conversations relate to gender and socially constructed views, particularly the restriction placed on men and free expression, which I will talk about later in the book.

How you feel, at its core, speaks to your mental and emotional state at any given moment of the day.

How you feel drives your next actions and decisions, whether tiny, short-term and mundane ones, or life-changing, monumental and spectacular ones.

How you feel reflects the body you're reading this book from, the relationships you're forming. Your behaviours. Your activities. Your passions and perils. Your ability to cope in healthy ways and your cognizance of unhealthy habits and self-sabotaging behaviours disguised as coping tools.

How you feel reflects life as you know it in this very second. It should never be understated. Everyone has Mental Health just as everyone has Physical Health. How you feel is linked to how you promote and take care of your Mental Health. This impacts personal and professional lives, alongside your core intentions. The path you choose will determine your success and impact on your overall health and well-being, leading to a preferred destination or 'dream life' of your choosing. Reaching this point makes it more possible to help others do the same.

## Mental Health Treatment: A Complicating History

As a mental health nurse in this modern age, I am thrilled at the progress we have made in applying the language, systems and resources to something we all have—mental health. But the evolution of psychiatry to even acknowledge mental health and some of the issues that can go along with it was quite slow. And dare I say, *maddening.*

The reality is that problems and disorders that we recognise today as categories of mental illness to talk about, analyse, diagnose, and treat, were virtually all considered madness in the $17^{th}$ century alongside constructions of reason and unreason; truth and untruth as symptoms of alternative meaning. The burden of caring for vulnerable individuals had remained with their families rather than the state, viewed as an individual problem rather than a societal one. The ways that people were defined as 'insane', the language used and their treatment is far removed from what is experienced today through a better understanding of mental health and modern families in general (Hodgkin, 2007).

Then came the 'madhouses', institutions, or asylums, for at least two centuries, that would separate the "mad" from the mentally fit of the community. From 1808, there were publicly funded 'pauper lunatic asylums' in England which were in place as a result of a parliamentary agreement and the building of them became compulsory in 1845—meaning that on the turn of the century there were over 100,000 people in England and Wales being housed in them (Historic England, 2019). Later, renamed as 'mental hospitals', if you look back over the records, far too often, the people institutionalised were women, deemed disobedient or unwanted by husbands who could afford the required doctors' signatures to enforce their imprisonment.

Reasons for admission to the asylums listed in the UK and the US included 'hysteria', 'grief', 'death of sons in war', 'laziness', 'politics', 'egotism', 'business nerves', 'hard study' and even 'novel reading'. Once inside, inmates had no way to fight for their release as patients could not appeal their detention, although a relative or friend could apply for them to be discharged if they confirmed proper care of the person upon their release. Sadly, some patients never left the asylums and after spending twenty years in institutions they were forgotten about and died without ever being released.

Medical training, governmental regulations and societal focus centred on the logistics and functionality of these institutions.

Institutions symbolised a loss of social skills, excessive restriction, human rights violations, and simply no opportunities for rehabilitation.

In actuality, the 297 classified forms of mental illness defined in the *Diagnostic and Statistical Manual* (DSM-5) or the guidelines in the World Health Organisation's (WHO's) International Classification of Diseases (ICD-10) that affect thinking, mood and behaviour, were not defined yet. For that reason alone, it was a dark period in history. I can't even begin to think about the number of people during those two centuries marked by "madness," who, if given proper treatment, didn't need to be locked away and could have gone on leading quality lives.

It was the birth of the National Health Service (NHS) in 1948 and the Mental Health Act in 1959, which began a health treatment and therapy revolution.

Fast-forward to *today.*

According to the World Health Organisation, 1 in 4 people in the world will be affected by mental or neurological disorders at some point in their lives. Around 450 million people currently suffer from such conditions, placing mental disorders among the leading causes of ill-health and disability worldwide. The Mental Health Foundation (2019) estimates 1 in 6 people experienced a common mental health problem in the past week.

Treatments are available, but nearly two-thirds of people with a known mental disorder never seek help from a health professional, although in the UK, GP practices, hospitals and health services are bursting at the seams as they attempt to manage the demands placed on them by whole populations. Stigma, discrimination and neglect prevent care and treatment from reaching people with mental disorders, says the World Health Organisation (2018).

Professionals within specialist mental health teams, community agencies, social workers, teachers, nurses, doctors, natural, prescribed and illicit medications, helplines, hotlines, recovery and retreat centres, employers, even phone apps and online self-help resources seek to address the many conditions presiding over our mental health globe today. Still, as WHO says, despite growing resources in the 21st century, many people are isolated and aren't getting the care they need. For some, with more debilitating conditions, they don't have the faculties to make a choice to obtain care. For others, thankfully they're not in madhouses, but they are imprisoned by their minds while their hearts suffer from loneliness and lost potential—at all ages.

In this book, I will be talking about the L.O.V.E Leadership as a model I have created through my life journey, taking into account my experiences and discoveries. I want to share it to enable anyone to conduct themselves as a leader, becoming the best version of themselves that they can be, which will impact on lives individually and improve business productivity. I will explore feelings and thoughts as they relate to our wellbeing and potential—individually and collectively. Mental health is the foundation of love and belonging. Both at home and in the workplace. However, as I've always claimed, 'before you can love another you must first learn to love yourself'.

I have been a Registered Mental Health Nurse for almost twenty years. I have applied my experience and services in various countries, clinics, and corporations. Since the larger portion of the adult world works more hours than they spend entrenched in their personal lives, how you operate in business is fundamental to mental health, wellbeing and vice versa. I have vast experience of working in companies which include Statutory Services, health, social care and education, Voluntary and Community Sector, charities and community interest companies, private health care and within corporate partnerships who consider this. My assessment is that two-thirds of people who need help are not seeking it. They're scared of being judged and discouraged from being open and honest. Perhaps they're not being asked how they feel with authenticity, even if they're showing signs of distress. They may be thought of as inadequate, weak or lazy if they need a "wellness day" or some time off of work to address personal areas of their lives which requires their input.

I have personal experience of this type of approach whereby as an employee with an impeccable attendance record, I spoke with my manager as I needed some short-notice leave to deal with a personal situation. My granddad had been into hospital to have a hip replacement and he had called me whilst at home because his mobility had deteriorated. My granddad never called me or asked for help. He comes from a generation where this wasn't how you did things and as I indicated before, this would not be considered how a man expressed himself, so I knew at the time it must be a desperate situation for him to contact me. As the only remaining family member to help him, following the death of my grandma, father and aunty in that order, I wanted to make sure he was okay and had everything he needed. At the time, he was in his eighties and continued to live in a flat independently. I was in a senior leadership position and had not been absent from work for over twelve years, in addition to regularly working above and beyond my contracted hours. I was in disbelief when my manager, who had initially told me to go and attend to my granddad, then demanded that I be back at work the following day and would mark me down as an unauthorised absence if I didn't arrive. I tried to explain the situation and was dismissed. I was even told that I would have to make up the missed hours the following week.

I remember feeling confused and upset. I knew what my manager was saying was incorrect and unreasonable, besides which my contract gave me up to five days' paid carers leave if I needed it and a very generous sickness pay scheme. I tried to speak with the organisation's HR department for advice, between the tears and emotions that filled me about my granddad's predicament. Here I was met with riddles and a lack of clarity or support, although I was informed that the manager's behaviour was unreasonable, which I was well aware of because in the whole of my career I had never responded to an employee in such a way. Being a conscientious employee who prided myself on good work, I returned to work the following day after I had rushed to try and put the support in place that my granddad needed. I spent the remaining two hours of the day in my office crying whilst trying to pull myself together. I was not productive for the business for that moment in time until I knew my granddad was okay.

The experience did provide me with confirmation of something though: I didn't actually matter to my manager or the business. It also gave me an opportunity to think more about my destiny.

Businesses are under pressure to compete and deliver and therefore needs all its resources at hand to achieve results. Mental health promotion may not seem like a priority to individuals or businesses, however, the negative impact of being unable to maintain good mental health can be seen in high sickness absences from work, unhappy people living unwanted lives and worse, people dying by suicide.

Whether it is an authoritative boss or an existing corporate culture that is high on pressure, low on empathy, a person in need of support is being additionally impacted upon by this environment. L.O.V.E Leadership can impact positively upon these situations by considering each of the areas and helping you put them into practice. I've lived by this model, and the experience related to my granddad's cry for help initiated my first step to doing more of what I loved and less of what I didn't. This also gave me the freedom to help others in a much more productive way. And here I am!

Equally important is the support for the children and young people who are growing up and will become people who work in and lead businesses. There are questions being asked about our teen population and whether they are being robbed of mental health care during their most impressionable years. If you have not seen the news or stories on social media you may be wondering 'How?' We've all been teens and I believe that early intervention is key in enriching the next generation to live happy, healthy and fulfilling lives. Children may or may not use the terms *stigma* and *discrimination*; however, the displays of such reaction to difference is demonstrated in the bullying and gang-related behaviours that happen.

Some young people have a deeper understanding of stigma and discrimination, which I have seen in my work when creating a "Mental Health 5 a Day", for and with children and young people, as part of a national project; however, we have all seen evidence that bullying of others takes place sometimes with extremely tragic outcomes that cannot be undone, which are magnified with the growing availability of social media, technology development and an apparent inability to distance or remove oneself from its impact (Ehmke, 2019). These behaviours are not exclusive to children and young people. Sometimes parents and carers are just as responsible for not supporting authenticity and individualism within their family units. I have seen this many times through my work in supporting educational institutes and families over the last two decades. It was the reasoning behind me developing a group programme for whole families called "SEA-ing Changes," which is jointly delivered between one of my companies, Arterne: Enriching the next generation CIC and Beach Schools South West CIC. I wanted to help families to work within their whole family system to effect changes to help improve lives and the outcomes for children and young people.

The significance of this approach is not always realised and as a result of my life and experience of working at a senior level within various Child and Adolescent Mental Health Services (CAMHS), it was not something I wanted to forget. This, coupled with promoting good mental health and addressing challenging behaviours through a structured activity-based group programme taking place on the beach, is a formula for success.

The process of encouraging children and young people outside of the classroom is phenomenal. I wrote the group programme with this in mind and knew the partnership between Arterne CIC and Beach Schools South West CIC to deliver the activities and interventions together would work well because of its non-traditional educational approach to impact positively within the family unit, increase environmental awareness and achieve academic improvement (functional skills). I was delighted that they accepted my proposal, and we have developed the programme from strength to strength, as an alternative to usual health and educational input, with successful results for families attending.

As our world becomes more connected, creative, culturally intertwined, gender-fluid, politically and religiously agnostic, it can seem that previous generations are struggling with change and the identity of the younger generations. This very visible struggle is indeed, sending a signal to our younger population that who they are blossoming into is not good enough or disruptive. Some families may not have aspirations and therefore, never encourage the younger generation to have any; other families may place so much pressure on their children to achieve academically or financially it limits the ability to be okay with oneself and their dreams. This perceived lack of acceptance and support can diminish someone's identity or the ability to remain mentally healthy, which can continue into adulthood.

Note that the U.S. Department of Health and Human Services (2017) indicate that half of all people with mental health disorders show first signs before a person turns 14 years old, and three quarters of mental health disorders begin before age 24. This is why it is essential to promote how important looking after your mental health and waking up happy in the life you want to live is significant. Once you've mastered this for yourself you can go on to help others achieve what that means for them.

To assist you I will share numerous examples of how scenes that shape, distort or strengthen our mental health play out in settings everywhere—I even include my own experiences and guide you on how L.O.V.E Leadership can impact positively for you at home and in the workplace.

I will talk about growing up and the developmental stage, transition in adulthood and business—three lifecycle markers in which our mental health and resilience is shaped differently.

By the time you are finished with *Draw a Heart Around It*, I hope you will internalise three truths about mental health that are sure to improve your outlook and inspire you to help others lead the life they want to live:

1.Many factors contribute to mental health problems, including:

- Biological factors, such as genes, physical illness, injury, or brain chemistry
- Life experiences, such as trauma or a history of abuse
- Family history of mental health problems

2. Studies show that people with mental health problems get better and many recover completely. Recovery refers to the process in which

people are able to live, work, learn, and participate fully in their communities.

3. When employees with mental health problems receive effective treatment, it can result in:

- Lower total medical costs
- Increased productivity
- Lower absenteeism
- Decreased disability costs

(Note: I did not create these truths. I'm simply echoing the U.S. Department of Health and Human Services here.)

Of course, the main purpose of the book is to share the model of L.O.V.E Leadership and to help you apply it in life and in business. The reason I laid out these truths is simple: If everyone on the planet understood this information, there would be no stigma or discrimination as it relates to mental wellbeing. If you have a brain and nervous system, you have mental health. If you have a heart, you have mental health. Like our physical anatomy, it's not "perfect". It is your birth right to implement tools and techniques that improve it. I want to add to that toolkit by sharing L.O.V.E Leadership with you.

Now, before I go any further on this path, combining deeply personal narratives and instruction, I must state that any recommendation herein is designed for those who may benefit from the L.O.V.E Leadership model, which I've spent many years developing and putting into practice. It is not meant to replace any active medical care or medication. This model requires active self-awareness and personal application that may not be possible within some mental health concerns that may require a specialist, treatment and intervention from a team of skilled and knowledgeable people. L.O.V.E Leadership describes a model that can be applied by individuals and organisations on a journey to learn how to conduct themselves as a leader of themselves and others. It's a journey toward a healthy and happy life. And a productive business. It will help you determine where you want to go and how you're going to get there—and staying focused on what you want to achieve.

## It's Your Mental Health, So Why Trust Me? Why L.O.V.E?

My mother is also a Registered Mental Health Nurse although this is not the reason I became one myself. I wouldn't say it's a case of 'Like mother, like daughter'. We have many differences and how we respond to and consider things does not align. I started training in 1997 after I fell into becoming a nurse quite accidentally. My own daughter was one year old at the time. I have clear memories of going to the interview and receiving the acceptance letter because they were significant milestones in my life. I had never thought my entry into university would be possible, as that is what I was told by the people educating me. It was a real achievement when I did succeed. Today, my daughter uses her creative skills as an actor and painter. Although she cares for people, she didn't want to go into the same profession as me. However, what we all have in common is that our personal, raw experiences have shaped our profession mostly.

I'm a lifelong student. I've worked hard and studied at the same time so that I could understand more about connecting and working with people to help make a difference. I've become an Eye Movement Desensitisation and Reprocessing (EMDR) therapist working with people who have experienced trauma and have Post Traumatic Stress Disorder (PTSD). I obtained a Master's degree in Professional Practice: Critical Issues for Practice Development and a Post Graduate Certificate in Transformational Leadership. I've qualified as a Non- Medical Prescriber, although I've spent more time focused on *non-medical* interventions to help support people. I've completed many other qualifications and had a variety of experiences over the years, all of which has assisted me to help myself and others. I also work as a National Consultant for STORM Skills Training CIC, focused on Suicide Prevention and Self-Harm Mitigation, which enhances skills to save lives. This is life-changing.

When people see my CV, they marvel at how many courses I've done! The truth is that I have a passion for learning, which is interesting given my secondary school experiences, as I left there with low self-esteem, low self-confidence and little belief in me as a person. I've studied extensively so that I can deliver excellent care and support those who have needed it. I've always seen the importance in investing in myself and my learning. I've never expected this to come to me free of charge, which is why I think I place value on it all. This education alongside my vast experiences have helped me to support myself and others. I have nothing to prove to anyone because I know I'm good enough, although this wasn't always the case. I am someone with a good heart and integrity—I like who I am and I've had to learn and practice believing and living that way, which has sometimes been easier said than done. I also need to regularly refresh my focus, which keeps me on track for having the life I want to live and making a difference to others.

The thing is, I didn't know I had to *learn* this; in fact, it never even crossed my mind. You can't know what you don't know; this is a 'blind spot', which is confirmed in 'The Johari Window Model' created by Luft and Ingham in 1955. Experiences and developing knowledge inform your thinking around gaining insight. I've been on a journey to learn that I am enough. I don't have to please anyone else. I often use an expression to say I'm like marmite: 'Love me or hate me', I am always me. Kind, caring, open-hearted and willing to help anyone. I love helping to encourage other people feel better, sharing unconditional love and making a difference. This does require honest communication from the heart, which is sometimes hard for people to consider or reflect upon.

This is where the development of L.O.V.E Leadership comes in. Once I had reached my destiny and I felt I was enough and living a life of happiness, doing more of what I loved and less of what I didn't, I wanted to share my message about how exactly someone else could take the same journey I had taken to freedom. L.O.V.E Leadership is a simple concept which uses LOVE as an acronym to provide a framework to guide travelling your journey. *Listen. Own. Voice. Empower.*

In this book, I will describe the model in detail and demonstrate how it can be applied every day. I firmly believe that it is an elixir for our mental health and choosing a quality life. I will give you examples of the absence of it and the havoc that has caused, including darker times in my own personal story. I'll teach you how each area of the model can free you, empower you and uplift you. I've also invited brilliant contributors, 'Wellness Warriors', to share their insight. By the time you finish *Draw a Heart Around It*, you'll be eager to draw your own heart—around your daily life and around the team or organisation that you lead.

It's all in your hands, and L.O.V.E Leadership can guide you in filling in the splendour of it.

# Chapter 1

## *From Conflict and Contempt to Bliss—The Model*

L.O.V.E LEADERSHIP IS A PERSONAL journey someone can take to self-actualisation: it is about psychologically moving from one place to another, which you may not always see as possible. This is often the reason that people become stuck in repeating patterns of behaviours where required changes do not occur, leaving things feeling like they're not improving or getting worse. Most importantly, it is about how you conduct yourself as a leader of *you*, as this will impact positively on every aspect of your life and the decisions you make.

In this book, I want to give you a shortcut about how to feel empowered, which will lead you to a happy life personally and professionally. I want to share my journey with you, the lessons I've learned for myself, and save some of that heartache—and headache—for you. I hope you will go on to do the same for others.

The first important message is that it's okay to be you. You must like you. You are enough. Believe in yourself. Anything is possible and you can achieve anything you put your mind to. I'm a great believer of 'you get out what you put in to something'. I've managed to achieve great things in my life and helped others to do the same.

L.O.V.E Leadership resonates with, helps individuals and changes the systems that we work in, because we *are* those systems. How we view things are what we will see show up. This is important to remember when thinking about our desired future.

In my various roles I work in health and social care settings, educational settings, corporate environments and I see people starting work on their emails at 6:00 in the morning (or earlier) and working until very late into the evening just because it's the only time they feel they can fit it in. This can sometimes lead to people missing out on doing the things that matter the most. I used to be that person feeling pressured to get everything done for fear of the consequences or being judged. The question is, why don't we take care of ourselves? How can we take care of other people and companies if we don't take care of ourselves? Do we ever consider that question? Self-care influences whether I'll have good relationships or bad relationships, how I raise my children, how I am in my job and what I'm willing to accept. Am I feeling empowered to prioritise the things in life that really matter to me? There has been increasing evidence and discussion about the use of mobile phones and social media upon human relationships which suggests we are losing our connectedness and forgetting how to prioritise what's of more value to us. Information has never been so freely available to us yet we choose to ignore the important messages within it and often say one thing and do another. Establishing your core intentions is essential.

I started my journey to freedom in my adult years and it took me until the age of 40 to know who I was and know that I am really okay; I am the epitome of the L.O.V.E Leadership model, so I know it works! This is what has equipped me to help others more effectively. For example, amidst a heavy work schedule and to test my self-esteem after years of employing L.O.V.E Leadership, I got into pole dancing as a hobby and exercise regimen. Then followed aerial hoop. I've also done trapeze and the silks. I do it to increase my fitness levels and take part in occasional photo shoots. I remember that in the beginning, I wasn't interested in doing photo shoots because I lacked confidence and worried about what people might say or how I may be judged. None of this is relevant to me now. I'm glad I did it, as I have some really great images that make me smile. I felt confident and empowered. I loved every moment of doing these hobbies and I met some wonderful women through it all. I was even a leader in creating a show to empower women alongside another women. We called it '*Elevate*'. I performed in the first show in 2017 with nine other women for the opening performance, which was a chair dance. I also performed a solo aerial hoop routine which I was coached for over the summer period prior to the event. I never thought I would have the confidence to do something like this and was motivated to demonstrate to others that it was possible regardless of age, size, shape or ability.

L.O.V.E Leadership supported this achievement and a 'Healthy Body: Healthy Mind' really is a winning combination. All of this reminds me of achieving and fully arriving as 'me' through L.O.V.E Leadership by:

- L.O.V.E. Listening actively
- L.O.V.E. Owning my stuff; remembering my roots
- L.O.V.E. Having a Voice and not being afraid to use it
- L.O.V.E. Empowering self and others through engagement and education to evolve

In order to make L.O.V.E Leadership real and manageable for you, it's important to trace your collective roots from the time we come into the world, through our developmental years, into adulthood and our professional lives. So much can go wrong amidst the twists and turns of life, but so much can go right, too, when we have the tools and opportunities which we have to create for ourselves. When we consider where we are, where we are going, why and how we are going to get there, amazing things can happen. L.O.V.E Leadership can help to guide us through.

## Listen

Listening to yourself and listening to other people are connected and like anything else, it is something which can be done well when practiced. When we are able to master 'listening' it is a powerful intervention and one that I place much value upon. Early experiences related to babies crying to communicate their needs for survival determine what happens next. Adults get attuned to what a baby is trying to communicate without the use of a single word. Babies are still able to get their needs met. Focusing on and understanding the communications between people and not waiting to fill a silence or jump into a gap in conversation with something you want to say, interpreting silence and use of body language and the unspoken word to know what is being communicated are important. To actively listen is the most utilised skill I have practiced both in out and of my employed positions. It is also one which anyone can do with practice.

*Actively listening* is empowering for self and others, especially when you're not using it to criticise yourself or blame self or others for failings. *Everyone* has an internal dialogue that they don't usually want to share with someone else. Learning when to listen to this or not is vital. How many times have you been asked a question and responded with the expected response rather than the one that comes from within? How many times have you heard that internal dialogue question your ability, your credibility, your accuracy and the person you are? Have you ever heard your internal dialogue tell you that you aren't enough, you're not good enough and people don't like you or don't want to hear what you have to say? Think about it for a moment.

Did it stop you from following your dreams? We all have built in physical feelings, which can be expressed and felt in our bodies, telling us a lot about ourselves or others. Some may describe this as intuition; others may have experienced something traumatic and some may have a good understanding of where and how physical and mental health meets. How much attention do people pay to that ache or pain that has become apparent or returned once again? How we listen and respond can be shaped and used to create a powerful interaction. What we do now is what we have learned and believe in. Listening to what someone is saying can be misinterpreted, too. It's harder for people to listen and make sense of things that they don't agree with. It's possible to project how you are feeling onto what someone is saying—a good example of this is with email communication; the intention of the email being sent may not be the perception of what is received. How is it possible to take a tone of email when we are talking about words on a page? It's all about interpretation and that is related to how someone feels about themselves. The important thing here is to decide who you are being when you're reading that email. *Listening takes practice.*

It's also easy to occupy your mind with the things you have left to do on your job list at work or the things you have to juggle in your personal life. What would happen if you created a list of what you are not going to do? Being distracted in communication means that you aren't able to actively listen. If you have ever experienced being listened to, you will understand how amazing it feels, how powerful it is. If you are someone who does not feel heard you will know how lonely that can feel.

All of this is also connected to the other areas identified in L.O.V.E Leadership.

## Own

'Owning your stuff' and 'remembering your roots' are phrases that resonate with me when I'm thinking about not forgetting where we have come from or the experiences that have shaped us. It's our story or narrative. I have heard other people refer to this as 'baggage'. Regardless of how it is defined what I am talking about here is the ability to recognise and shape *you* using your experiences, their interpretation and family culture. This is about awareness and just knowing who you are being in any given situation. Exploring and understanding reactions, behaviours and conversations. Moving away from negativity and stepping toward positivity, which I have seen and helped many people to achieve when they have been struggling to find clarity.

This "help" had to begin with me. I didn't have this developed thinking when I was growing up—at times it felt like everything was negative and people were "against" me. I eventually recognised that this thinking was as a result of my mother's influence and belief system, which was based on her life experiences. This is not my story to tell; however, it is partly what has shaped me before my journey, alongside my dad's life experiences. What I believe is their attempts to raise me was with the best intentions and using the knowledge and skills they had at the time.

Understanding the impact of generations, extended family, parents, carers or guardians, siblings, culture upon you as an individual is meaningful in who you become. You may not deem it as an important consideration and often we become blind to its significance. What I would say to you is don't deny it. Don't attempt to forget it. You're taking ownership of your history, your 'baggage', your story. To accept where you came from or what your patterns have been is to learn how far you've come once you've gained traction to better life and health. Ownership is about minimising the 'load' that you carry through life's journey, how long this goes on for and whether experiences can be reframed to promote an alternative impact on an individual or situation. It can also determine your chosen destination in life.

Repeating patterns of behaviour are a challenge that people may need help to recognise and alter to achieve a different experience and outcome, or otherwise remain stuck in them. An example of this for me has been related to relationships and particularly my choice in men. My truth is, I've been in many abusive relationships of varying degrees. I didn't always know this at the time; however, when I did, it was something that I felt ashamed of because I felt inadequate and deserving of their treatment or punishment. Like all forms of abuse, our dirty, little secret remained unexposed out of some unhealthy sense of loyalty or invisible promise to the abuser that could not be broken for fear of discrediting them or tarnishing their character. I'm an incredibly loyal person. This meant that I suffered, in silence, at their hands.

There is no doubt that these life choices stem from my earlier experiences, family cultures and something you can read about in various books and journal articles about *attachment* discussed by Ainsworth, (1973); Bowlby, (1969); and Holmes, (2001). I also know its impact on every aspect of an individual's life, which is why gaining insight is so valuable for someone. People feel confused about themselves and don't always feel comfortable with who they are. This can prevent some people from achieving their full potential. No one said it was easy!

It is possible to achieve and it will shape the decisions you make; who you are in life and who you are in business.

There were many relationships, including friendships, which were not healthy for me whilst I was growing up. Friendships were determined by what I could do for them or how I could make them look or feel.

Through my teenage years, I gained attention from men of all ages. Between 14 and 15 years old, I was part of a group of young people who hung around with older men. Looking back at that time I realise that this was a strange situation as were some of my experiences. I remember a man, aged 29, who wanted to kiss me, succeeding on a few occasions and wanting to pursue a relationship with me, which was encouraged by other members of the group. I wasn't attracted to him and I'm now aware that it was my vulnerabilities that attracted him to me. At this time, there were other experiences that were worse. A man from the same group, who was five years older than me, also pursued a relationship with me. This is not something I wanted to be involved in, it just happened. This man had sex with me without consent on numerous occasions. I didn't resist it. I just froze. I was physically present and psychologically disassociated. I didn't have my voice about this and it didn't stop until I moved on from that time in my life. The #MeToo campaign has again highlighted to me how many people stay quiet about these things for so long. I know it is even harder for men to speak about their experiences. It's just not something you want to tell people about and I've had to work through this for myself.

Campaigns like #MeToo connect to L.O.V.E Leadership by using people's experiences to empower them and not define them. This was true for me and impacts positively on my mission to help others to live the life they want.

It's also true that some people can just pick out a victim to prey on. I do believe that there have been times in my life where I have repeated the pattern and been a victim for people to take advantage of at various times, which has continued into my adult years whilst I didn't address it.

I was married to someone who was much older than I was and he treated me with disrespect. The experience had a big impact on me and I lost my identity, my voice, my confidence, my worth, my self-esteem and self-respect as he chipped away at my character. I faced physical and sexual abuse at his hands, as I was made to engage in things that I didn't want to do. I had an internal dialogue that criticised and blamed myself and looking for reasons that confirmed his actions towards me and made me " to blame" or "deserving" of what he dished out.

There is information to suggest that working in mental health attracts and employs a large number of people that are on a journey or who need to start a journey, whether that is known or unknown. In my opinion, I was one of those people! It's easy for me to recognise and say out loud now. I have met people through my work from all industries and seniorities that I have supported over the years. I learned that there were lots of people that were just like me, who struggled with similar things; some still do and they just needed some help to live a better life. My experiences of this have been positive and negative. I guess what I'm saying here is that it isn't always an easy road to take. However, it is possible, and experience can help build resilience in you. Humans like to sit in comfort zones and fear the unknown.

I think your experience depends on the risk you're prepared to take yourself and defines whether it becomes something worthwhile or not. I believe this is true for any person in any job role, anywhere.

## Voice

Have a 'voice' and don't be afraid to use it; however, recognise that if this is good for you it is also good for other people which is why it's strongly connected with 'listen' within the L.O.V.E Leadership model. Having a voice also includes where that voice is being communicated and how. Discussing things that may leave people feeling uncomfortable is one of the reasons why individuals, work colleagues, teams, services or systems don't open communications to include support and challenge. This isn't about having the loudest voice or being right—this is about being able to manage conversations or situations in a respectful and professional way. Take the team who are unhappy about the cleanliness of the kitchen in their office base. Each team member will have an opinion about the state of the kitchen, where and how they voice that is likely to differ. This impacts on behaviour and ultimately the productivity of the business. I've worked in teams where people have refused to clean the kitchen because it isn't their mess, yet at the same time, they have been unwilling to talk directly with the person they think is making the mess about how it is leaving them feeling in favour of gossiping about that person to another team member. You can see why this approach isn't conducive to good team work or business productivity. Nor does it assist someone to reach their desired lifelong goal.

Feelings of fear can be a driver in determining when and how people use their voice. For example, I have worked in a lot of organisations that are regularly inspected by regulators or monitors. The process of inspection quite often leaves people feeling vulnerable, which is enhanced if the inspection doesn't feel like it is going well. In order to appease inspectors, organisations will select the truth or shape it so that they can be seen in a much more positive light by the inspectors. This does little to serve or benefit the people using the services. However, the consequences of not achieving what inspectors want is deemed so significant that people are encouraged to tell them what they want to hear. The power imbalance creates a vulnerability and an expectation that people will not say anything that will compromise the company.

For anyone wanting to discuss things openly and honestly it is possible that you will find yourself in a minority or labelled as a trouble maker if you go against an agreed version of events. I've seen people fall foul to this numerous times. Organisations benefit from creating a culture that goes beyond groupthink and one which supports individuals to use their voice, even when what they are saying may be challenging to hear. Here, I want to acknowledge that I did have a few role models who helped me see the contrary of groupthink: Deanna always knew what to do and helped to guide me when I needed it; Phil was a fabulous mentor and helped shape my nursing skills; and Cate inspired me to keep innovating.

One simple exercise, 'The Constructive Rant' can help teams and was something introduced to me by Professor Steve Onyett, who focused his latter practice on interdisciplinary team work and its enhancement using solution-focused approaches to mutual support and change (Onyett, 2007). It gives teams a structured way to regularly speak about things they are unhappy about in a time limited period. This then helps to move to the problem-solving stage. I recall a team that were introduced to this exercise because they had gotten into a position where they were negative about everything in their working environment. It was a very small team and they just couldn't find a way of speaking with one another openly. They would all talk to me and colleagues about each other to blame and complain which wasn't conducive to good team working. The team meeting had a section for the Constructive Rant and initially produced a forty-five minute discussion focused on everything that was wrong, which is exactly what they were doing on a day-to-day basis. As the weeks went on, trust was built, the conversations about what was wrong became less and less so much so that they wanted to withdraw 'rant' from the meeting. I supported their decision somewhat reluctantly and guess what happened? In no time at all they were back to having conversations in secret about each other, which were problem focused and promoted mistrust.

How people lead themselves is significant in whether they can find happiness in their personal or professional lives. People need to get into the right mind-set. People need to be honest.

There have been times in my life where I have lost my voice. When I re-learned to use my voice, let alone recognising that I still had one prior to that, I felt more solid, more whole, more present, more independent, happier, and healthier. It took time and required me to take risks both personally and professionally. I am someone who has always prided myself on doing the right thing. I believe in acting with integrity and being honest. Even if I have been afraid or the only person to speak up I have continued to do the right thing. Some people doubt this because it's not always an easy thing for people to achieve. There have been many occasions where I have spoken as a lone voice where I've known that others have decided not to say anything for fear of the consequences for them. This has left me vulnerable at times, yet I have remained true to myself and doing the right thing in serving others. It does take strength and courage. And practice! I've always believed that acting with integrity is saying and doing the same thing even when no one is looking. What does it mean to you?

I lost my voice on more than one occasion, both in my personal life and professional life. I had to rebuild my confidence to change this and make some life decisions to support my journey destination. I am so pleased that I was able to do this and I am literally an open book now because I feel okay with myself. Realising that you have a voice, even when that doesn't feel true, is a step to take towards empowerment and living the life you want. This is my reason for sharing L.O.V.E Leadership with you all.

## Empower

Empowerment is connected to all other areas of L.O.V.E Leadership. Through listening, owning and voice, I learned how to empower all people, especially women. As a testament to this, in 2018, I was nominated and selected as a semi-finalist in the Devon and Cornwall Venus Awards in the UK. It was unexpected and nice to be nominated and chosen to be in the top 5 women for 'Influential Women of the Year'. There were so many wonderful women associated with these awards it was a fantastic thing to be involved in and I would recommend that women take part in the Venus Awards wherever they can because it promotes the celebration of women's achievements by everyone, which is very special.

Empowerment does have to start from within you. It is about engagement and education of self and others. It's about intention and heart. Engagement is made easier through listening. This has to be genuine interest in another human being and isn't always only about the spoken word. It's about listening to what's right for you. Within companies engaging is about also including the voice of people to shape company culture and development. Transparency is vital and open, honest communications that will be listened to have the greatest impact in engaging with employees and other stakeholders. This is linked also to acting with integrity. This is an easier interaction when individuals feel empowered themselves. It brings greater levels of self-esteem and confidence in being yourself, which everyone struggles with at times.

Stepping into the shoes of another is not always something that is obvious. It is something I promote within everything that I do; this supports me to continue to promote and spread unconditional love. Education of self and others supports the journey to empowerment. I believe in educating hearts. People will judge themselves and others. They may criticise and blame unconsciously. Gossip is destructive and does not empower people. It is different to someone having a voice and the only way to deal with it is to challenge it at the time and make it clear that you do not want to take part in it; otherwise, you risk cliques forming, which can be unhealthy.

I've been challenged in this view numerous times, and my response is always one that reminds people that they are individuals with choices. Leaders shouldn't be ostracised because of their job role. They are human beings too and often trying to do a challenging job. This is empowerment and intentions behind actions, conversations or behaviours are best when they are heartfelt and caring. Education of self and others is an on-going process and one which requires people to be open to an alternative view. These things collectively support people to evolve and they take practice. It's important to remember that you cannot determine or control what others say about you. This needs to be left behind. It's insignificant on your journey.

Surround yourself with people who will help you to create a positive energy and experience. You will soon be at your desired destination.

# Chapter 2

## *Ice Cream and Impressions: Through a Child's Eyes*

As we examine where we are in life and if we don't like what we unravel, it's important to remember that our early decisions and vulnerabilities were as innocent children first. Did we develop fully? Positively? With aspirations?

The answer will be different for everyone. The answer may still be in the discovery phase. Regardless, we all have the opportunity to reach a fulfilling life and achieve our goals.

I was seven when I tried to run away from home for the first time. I grew up on a council estate, social/low-cost housing built by the government in the UK and Ireland; "council housing". My parents were quite young when they had me, which was expected soon after marriage at the time. As I mentioned, I was the oldest of three children. My mum was 20, my dad almost two years older. They had different upbringings. My mum was brought up predominantly by my gran who had children out of wedlock with my granddad, which was unique for the time. My dad was brought up by his parents and lived with them and his younger sister, a family of four, as a much more traditional 'nuclear' family unit.

Recognised in the work I do with individuals and families, these things are relevant to who I am and how I developed, which is true for everyone and perhaps not enough attention is paid to this when contemplating direction and desires.

Financially it was always difficult. Both of my parents wanted the best for their children doing the best they could with the skills and knowledge they had.

If I think about my dad and describe him, he was a very honest man. Fiery. In my time, I've had some of these traits, too! I'm much calmer now. My profession has helped me with this. Growing up, I was much like him—honest, blunt and fiery. He also had a good sense of humour and knew how to have fun. Lots of people have used the phrase, "you're just like your dad". My dad was very authentic. He was what he said he was. If he was angry, you got anger. If happy, you got his happiness. He didn't hold grudges. He was not complicated in that sense. Strong work ethic. He always taught me that being honest was important and not forgetting your roots. I'm not quite sure that he meant this in the same way as I refer to it in my L.O.V.E Leadership model!

When I speak at conferences or events, I tell the audience that I was reliably informed by my parents that I was seven years old when first I tried to leave home.

So the story goes: In my dressing gown, I packed my bag and took it to the front door, let myself out, walked up the street because I'd decided I was going to go to the local supermarket precinct area to sleep there for the night. That seemed like the best thing to do. Looking back, that was a way of expressing that I wanted something different, as children often do through their behaviour. My parents always talked about wanting to have a better life: education and opportunities for the children. Their need for my better-ness didn't actually include me. They didn't communicate with me. I ended up living with my aunt and uncle at a challenging time for any child aged 10, going home at weekends only, until the house sale and move was completed. I was moving from primary school to secondary school—year six, going into seven in England, attending a school where I didn't know anyone and at a crucial time in a child's development (Morgan, 2013; Saffran, 2003). I can't even remember saying goodbye to my friends.

## Mysteries of the Teenage Brain

As a young person, you are going through lots of changes, you have physical development, belonging, teenage brain development, identity, sexuality, relationships. I talk with young people and parents/carers about teenage brain development a great deal in my work as a nurse because it is so significant in how we develop into adults. I was informed about this or given an opportunity to discuss it with anyone.

From a social perspective, during the move I was going to a school with higher-quality education; the trouble with that was highlighted in me being 'rough around the edges'! I wasn't the same as other students. As kids in the council estate, we sorted things out by fighting in the street or the car park. No one tried to help me understand this situation. All I knew was I was different and didn't fit with what seemed to be the norm.

Growing up without means, I didn't really have aspirations. I do remember thinking that I wanted to be a vet or an airline hostess, but this never went further than a fleeting thought. I never thought about being a nurse. Like I said before, I fell into being a nurse, which was after my daughter was born. I knew I enjoyed helping people, which had started in my early teens.

I eventually left home at fifteen. This was after I had been running away a lot over a period of years. I had good cause in my mind at the time. I recall that was a very challenging time for me and my parents, which was a different sort of challenge that I had experienced previously whilst growing up. Like any ordinary adolescent I was working out who I was, taking risks and transitioning into adulthood. Amongst many other things, I dyed my hair red, which was opposed by my grandmother, Dad's mum, who was very traditional. She had exasperated, "You can't do that!" I had been running away also, and she said I was shaming the family name. My response was simple: I said I would change my name then! I was outspoken for a teenager, deep down I wasn't happy. I always had spirit. I also had times where life felt terrible for me and I had brief interactions with social care.

I'm not sure any of it was channelled in the right way and I lacked emotional intelligence. Things were never discussed with me, partially because my parents didn't have the understanding and partly because their own experiences of being parented were limited to the existing family culture.

They had a particular way of understanding how families are brought up, which was rigid and strict. I wouldn't go as far to say that there was a belief that children should be seen and not heard; however, at times, it came close. My mother's upbringing was fairly relaxed in some ways, maybe too relaxed. There was contact between the children and their father; however, I've been told that his absence from the family home was better as the relationship with their mother was volatile. Her upbringing also lacked the relationship you would expect to see between a mother and her children, which at times meant there was a role reversal whilst the children became the adults and caretakers. I guess this goes some way in understanding my non-existent relationship with my mother now.

My daughter has a lot of spirit. She always has and this is what I've loved about her. I've embraced this spirit. More importantly, I have provided her with opportunities and information that enabled her to know about life and aspirations, which was a different to my upbringing. My family were very supportive in helping me to bring up my daughter, especially in those early years when I was studying and working two jobs to stay afloat. Initially, I brought my daughter up in the way in which I had been raised which was what was expected of me. This didn't feel right so I changed it. I told my daughter to do what made her happy and follow her dreams, which led her to attend New York Film Academy to continue her studies as an actor. My daughter...living in New York City for a year at the age of 21! I'm very proud of her. What an achievement!

As I put the final touches to this book, she is 23, living and working on an island just off of the mainland of Queensland, Australia. She is really enjoying it and continuing to live a life that brings her happiness. Long may it continue! There is nothing more important to me in my whole world than my daughter. This will not come as a shock to my husband. This is my benchmark for providing care and support to others. If it isn't good enough for my daughter then it's not good enough for anyone else.

Laurie and her generation is the nucleus of mental wellbeing as it more readily embraces all that L.O.V.E Leadership has to offer. Authenticity, diversity and inclusion, expression, and purpose are more regularly the staples of their identity. Here is how Laurie defined mental wellbeing and life goals:

"As my mum taught me, never settle for less or let anybody make you feel like you're not worth anything and if they do, get rid of them. You are worth it. Be confident in yourself. People have up and down days, which is totally normal, which she has also taught me. It's perfectly normal to feel rubbish on one day but to stay positive. You also need to respect yourself before others will respect you, and if they don't, you can't beg them to stay. They're not meant to be in your life. You don't need that kind of negativity. Regarding your family, they say your family is your family so you have to stick around, but I actually think if people are making you feel something in a negative way, you want to distance yourself, even if relatives. Know your self-worth, and don't let anyone put you down.

"Everyone has a part to play in mental health. People suffering with depression and anxiety don't know who to talk to, even today. There needs to be more reaching out to these people. They might not want to go visit somebody. They might not want to leave the house to seek that help. We need other options. People could get nervous on the phone as well, but it could be a good thing to have others go to people's houses or have a texting system in which they can anonymously seek help.

"My mum has been a nurse for a long time and she's always tried to approach mental health in different ways. I'm quite creative, so for me, what helped me in situations was being able to express myself through creating things rather than saying, this is what is wrong. I do a lot of painting, acting, performance, which makes me feel good, as it allows others to see my expression, which makes them feel good, which makes me feel better. Different options are important. Recognise that the one thing you may be doing for someone in need though well-intended is not doing the job. I'm very creative, so what works for me may not work for someone more intellectual and who might prefer to go on a more logical route. They may have to write their feelings down rather than talk to someone. Everyone needs to know that it's normal to get help, and your situation is not forever. Especially when someone is depressed, they may want to be alone due to shame. Having someone reach out to them would get a more positive reaction and successful outcome."

I've tried to show Laurie that she doesn't have to feel restricted by me. My upbringing was very restrictive and controlled and I rebelled against that. I can recall being brought home a couple of times by the police which were mainly related to me running away. It was all about expressing who I was. I never took trouble to my family home. I did associate with people who did, although I mostly made choices that kept me on a good path for my future. When I didn't it was also useful not to get caught!

I'm in no doubt that my Dad loved all of his children and applied the same skills of parenting that he was brought up with. I do remember being smacked. It was the way it was back then. I also recall being threatened and chased with a bamboo stick by my mother, which is not something that would be tolerated in our current society. My daughter and I laugh about it now because I can count on one hand the amount of times I smacked her as a child before I realised it wasn't going to work. I didn't like how it made me feel or the impact it was having on my daughter. The thing is, you do what you're brought up to do. Smacking and shouting was part of what our family did when I was growing up. I didn't know there was another way. These experiences can shape you. I was smoking cigarettes at age eleven and drinking alcohol at age twelve. There were others that did this, too. I didn't have anyone to talk to about life. My life could have ended up so differently and I often say that I am someone who is 'against all odds'.

I left school at fifteen as well. I did get my GCSE grades, which weren't expected if you listened to the reports of some teachers. I completed them with the required A-C grades; in my situation that was five Cs and a B, which gave me the entry and qualification to go into nursing in my adult years. I had very low self-esteem, low self-worth, and a lack of confidence. The school supported those pupils who they thought would do well and that wasn't me. I was angry, I broke rules, had a troubled home life—all which was far too much inconvenience for the school to deal with. I recall that they wanted to put me on a behaviour bond—to come back to school at sixteen to attend the sixth form. I didn't want to sign, so I ended up going to college where I got around 90 percent of absences on a health and social care course. There was a time when my parents didn't speak to me at all because I was the black sheep and in their eyes I brought heartache and upset to the family. I had two younger sisters. I remember going to take my youngest sister, Lucy, a Christmas present. My mother shut the door in my face, believing that I was claiming benefits and saying she didn't want my presents with "their money". That was an awful experience at around 16 or 17 years old.

From Mum's perspective, I had abandoned them all. She was bitter and negative, which I mimicked until I learned another way. It took me a while to realise those things and I didn't want my daughter to experience the same things from me.

Here, I want to bring in my sister, Lucy, to give more context on our upbringing from her perspective. Using my own background as the example, I want to underscore that mental health directly takes into consideration, family history and life experience such as early trauma. It is not to shame my family and I did consider leaving some of the details that my sister recalls out of the book altogether, I did not because they are her words, which she found hard to find. I found reading her words emotional as I had not heard them in this way before. Her words are used to illustrate where I came from, where my parents came from, with the next couple of chapters showing my direct evolution, through L.O.V.E Leadership. No one's upbringing is without trials and tribulations no matter what class, race or any tick-box category; we can all offer empathy around that basis, which is the building block for love and belonging.

**Lucy:** "Basically on the outside looking in, my upbringing was classed as a traditional working-class family. Mum, dad and two sisters (Cindy and Kerry).

"'Lovely children and parents,' 'Such a lovely family' are phrases I remember hearing from others. We dare not step out of line or say something our parents didn't want to hear or else we'd be in for it.

"After my big sister (Cindy) left home at an early age (I must have been 9) things became hard. I was left to think Cindy didn't want to know us, but as I got a bit older I realised this wasn't the case. Cindy had tried to see me and ring me but this was stopped by my mum. In fact, Cindy wasn't allowed to see me by say so of my mum. I missed my sister but didn't know what really was going on! I was just fed a load of one-sided bull, which back then, I was gullible to believe but in actual fact I was used like a chess piece by my parents. My middle sister, Kerry, was put into care due to her own lies. I was about 11 at the time when I broke down in front of my parents because I was being bullied by my sister Kerry's twin friends. We had to move due to the length of time the bullying went on for.

"I started trying to run away from home, and just got a whack when I did come home and got called selfish. Funny really!

"After that, things got really bad and I guess my parents gave up on parenting. Dad would work all the time and mum was all about her studies. I would always be getting in trouble with the police, drinking and taking drugs. Looking back, all I wanted was support and for someone to get involved, but I slipped through the net. Unfortunately, this happened a lot back then, simply brushed under the carpet!

"The situation with Kerry changed my Dad and he started drinking a lot. Sometimes I would get something chucked at me usually on the head, because I was trying to stand up for myself when he was saying something horrible. So, basically I was left to feel neglected and totally struggling with depression. I try to forget all my so-called 'foundations' of my life. I hated childhood. There were some good times like our holiday to Greece, but unfortunately, the bad outweighs the good.

"Two main memories of Cindy stick out to me: When my dad caught my sister in a boy's car, he was spying through the curtains and saw her get out of it. I was told to get upstairs, but unfortunately, heard everything. Dad was shouting and there was banging. I can't be sure what happened but I think my dad had hit my sister on her head with his fist. She had a big 'egg' on the front of her head the next day. When I went downstairs the next morning, in the kitchen I noticed there were ring marks where I learned that my sister Cindy was dragged around catching her jewellery on the magnolia painted walls. I never understood how he got away with this abuse. I never looked at my dad the same after that. I was terrified of him. That was just before she moved out.

"The second memory, which is a total contrast, was when she gave me away to my husband, Lee. If I didn't have her, God knows where I would be! She's my rock and in actual fact, she planned my whole wedding when she knew I was struggling.

"Cindy is such an amazing person, from when she left home to what she is today, I'm so proud of her. Cindy worked from nothing to be a powerful, professional woman, who has such a big heart and a lot of compassion within mental health, homelessness, youth, adults and the list goes on."

"With regards to my perspective on mental health well, as I have suffered with depression for many years, I feel people should talk more about it, in particular within the educational setting. Deteriorating mental health is not something to be ashamed of. It doesn't make you weak if you struggle with mental health issues.

"Cindy is such a dedicated professional, sister, mother. She spreads a lot of love and positivity whether in a professional setting or a personal setting. People can learn a lot from Cindy as I have."

## Reflection From the Heart

Lucy is seven years younger than me, so I was fifteen when what she described happened. Even though I know children hear stuff (and I have a deeper understanding now due to my job), I just didn't put those pieces together then. The ring marks on the wall; wow, I didn't expect that detail. She knew more than an inkling that something had happened. I remember that evening. My mother's words to me were, "Get out before he kills you," and that was the parting from my family at the time. I set off in the world. I never held a grudge; I learned forgiveness. That's a really important thing in life to learn. I made amends with my dad—he wasn't a bad man—he just didn't know what to do with his frustrations. The false accusations that another sister said about him had a lasting negative impact. She will have to come to terms with that.

I always knew Dad loved his children. He used to say to us, 'I love every hair on your head'.

My understanding about childhood experiences and families is vastly different now. My dad was only equipped with the skills because of his upbringing. The one thing I always knew about him was that he was very proud. He always told me how proud he was of us and that he loved us. His bad behaviour sometimes came from frustration with his own life. It may sound strange, he was the more caring parent, there's a lot about me that had to live up to his expectations. I was the oldest, and he had wanted a boy. This is how I was raised. If you were hit, you had to hit back, you had to stand up for yourself and fight for what you believed in. Stand up to bullies, starting with the biggest one. And I did.

## WELLNESS WARRIOR

### Wendy Hannon, Operations Manager, Hamoaze House

The first thing Wendy, a colleague for more than fourteen years, will tell you about me is that I have a depth of understanding of some of the issues people face, I always put a positive spin on things geared toward the solution and never the problem. I try to be very motivational in that respect. What I find motivational about Wendy is that she has exceptional wisdom about changing mental health and substance misuse treatment across the spectrum of care and she is candid in sharing it to stakeholders.

When I first met her at work, she was a commissioner for drugs and alcohol and I worked in the acute admission hospital as part of a team detoxing people from substances. We had these things called drug and alcohol action teams which purchased treatment options for people. It was a partnership between public health, police and probation, trying to work with people affected by problematic substance use initially in a way that was not just about criminalising them; it was trying to look at the reasons why they were using drugs and treating people for illness rather than treating them as bad people and punishing them for behaviours. That resonated with where I came from in terms of my own belief system. I worked with this group of people for some time and already knew that they weren't the bad people in society. They may have experienced bad things and done things that people could not understand, which often were related to what happened to them as children and carrying that into their adult lives. Case in point: my childhood!

Here, Wendy sat down to answer a few tough questions as a key partner in supporting the work of my company.

**Q: From a mental health perspective, what are we not getting as a society when it comes to treating depression and decreasing the rates of suicide?**

**A:** Fundamentally, I think about schools. Part of what we do where I work is partner with the schools and work with children who are excluded from other schools because of their behaviours. You just know that at 14 or 15, their lives will be really hard because their mental health is poor. A lot of that is anxiety and stress. We seem to be really good at piling on stress. While schools talk about doing mindfulness, we still put children under huge pressure to perform on exams and do a lot of activities. We also have social media where you can never walk away from a bully. I was reflecting with someone the other day about school. I was bullied in school because I had red hair and teeth that stuck out so I was a natural target. At least when I left school and went home for the weekend that was it until the following week. Nowadays, young people can never get away from it. They can't stop looking at their phones either and if they're not getting messages they don't think they're important. Then they get messages that are really negative. It worries me.

**Q: What I'm hearing from you is the need for more traditional connection?**

**A:** Yes, it's about people. Communication. When you're on text, you don't see facial expressions, the love in someone's eyes, or the happiness or the anger. You don't see any of that. Actually walking the streets and meeting the people is putting yourself out there as a real person and not just a telephone number. I admire it.

When I first heard the L.O.V.E Leadership terminology, I thought...okay, but with Cindy, it represents the person she is, so I get the model. She means it. She exudes LOVE and it's about all we've got really. When I look at the world, I get sad! I look at politics in the U.S. in horror—and not that it's any better in the UK! When you see this across Europe and America, there is this huge rise of the right wing when really, we need to start caring about people.

**Q: Is technology getting us more off the mark of just being human?**

**A:** Like anyone else, I see all the benefits of technology. You can get information, make contact. It's fantastic, but I've watched my own daughter, who is 29, and she can't put her phone down. It's like if it's not stuck to her, she's stressed out! Technology does larger things. I've watched my 6-year-old granddaughter, crying for my "iPad, iPad, iPad!"

## Reflection From the Heart

Just in that short snippet, Wendy talks about the ages of 6, 14, and 29. Each is astoundingly impressionable. The 6-year-old is forming her mental health based on experiences, make no mistake, it's a crucial time in life.

*Sticks and stones.* What all of this means is throughout our childhood, our adult selves are being formed. Our experiences shape us and how we become resilient or not determines our future life choices. There are endless books; journal articles; theories about all of this. Harvard University's Center on the Developing Child focuses a lot on how early experiences shape the architecture of the developing brain and lay the foundation of sound mental health; disruptions to this developmental process can impair a child's capabilities for learning and relating to others—with lifelong implications. Risk and resilience is important to consider in everything that happens as we develop in life. As is how we try and alleviate pain in order to make sure it's not approached with the wrong thing that may have a further negative impact.

Physical and mental health is important in equal measures. You can learn to pick yourself back up again. How an individual's development and mental health is nurtured is so imperative and how early you can intervene where there have been life experiences and events which have been negative, the better the quality of life growing up and transitioning into adulthood. I started working with adults initially. I saw them and their experiences show up in their behaviours as adults and I kept thinking, *Why didn't someone get to them earlier? What took so long in them getting or accessing help?*

That is what led me to start working with children and young people, believing that earlier intervention would minimise problems developing further and give people opportunity to address things in order for them to have a positive impact. Mind-set is equally important in what happens to how we develop and the decisions we make.

# Chapter 3

## *Dates with Danger*

THERE ARE CONSEQUENCES OF LOW self-esteem and low self-worth in children. I played out a lack of self-confidence through falling victim to abusive relationships in my personal and professional life. Trauma, such as that night my sister remembers vividly, traversed into patterns of behaviour and intergenerational, culture, and systemic issues that crisscross people and companies.

With these intricate and negative patterns, whole system approaches are required to counter them (more to come on that in Chapter 6).

It's true: I dated abusive men. This is a pattern that had played out for most of my life. The abusers wore many different disguises and were always very charismatic, all with their own stories that shaped who they became. Pre-marriage, as an adolescent, I experienced behaviours towards me from adult men that were unacceptable and abusive. I did not interpret these things in this way at the time. I was someone different to who I am today. I allowed things to happen, which I would not accept now. Then there were other longer term relationships; these experiences shaped me in a way that allowed me to continue to face the wrath of men psychologically and physically.

My first marriage was to an abusive man. We met through our shared profession, which made it more of a challenge to understand his behaviour. Looking back, I now know that his friendship, charm and charisma was the show in which he would catch my attention. He told me of a failing marriage and an abusive wife, which seemed like a credible story at the time. The fact was that he was very abusive—to me and his previous wife, whom he had two children with. She told me her story years later when we met at a women's night out and both in healthier relationships. Something she said to me that night rang true; she knew that if she had tried to tell me or warned me about him, I wouldn't have believed her. I knew she was right about this. It's true for lots of other people in similar situations. We can see perpetrators as victims because we want to believe what we are told, particularly in new romances, rather than exploring it further and checking our own lenses in which we see things.

I was 25 and he was 38 when we got married. He was very controlling and insecure. There are numerous examples of this behaviour going beyond an acceptable level for anyone. He would do things like drive to my workplace if I was not home on time. We worked in the same building for different teams. If I was late because I had been unable to leave a busy hospital ward, which happened frequently, I would go out to the car to find that he had put a note under my windscreen wipers, saying "Late again!" which actually meant he had driven from our home to my workplace, perhaps with the children, to intimidate me by leaving his note. He did this many times. In fact, restricting my time outside of the family home was a common feature throughout our relationship.

I was petrified of this man and didn't even wear makeup or nice clothes because he would accuse me of flirting with people. I remember he went to my male friend's house once because he had seen us outside the hospital together having a cigarette break. He visited him early on a Sunday morning to tell him to stay away from me. The controlling increasingly got worse over a short amount of time. I even recall him feeling jealous of someone riding past me on a motorcycle because I had commented on how much I had liked the bike. Then came the physical and psychological abuse. He would spit in my face and drag me around by my hair. He would call me names and tell me people didn't like me. He was a vile man. In this situation, mental abuse far outweighed the physical abuse.

He told me I was fat and that everyone talked about me. I was totally deconstructed. I never talked to people about it though. I didn't want to cause him an issue and believed his promises about changing. It added to my previous experiences. It took me a long time to bounce back from all of these experiences. I'd completely lost my identity. We had originally met whilst training as mental health nurses and became really good friends. We both had different relationships then and I can honestly say that I never saw us together; I just wasn't attracted to him and believed he was my friend. I wasn't aware of the details at the time. I later learned that he had basically warned someone I was having a casual relationship with that I "didn't want to see him anymore" (Hilarious, right?).

When I look back now, he was a perpetrator looking for a victim. And this is key when we talk about how our early childhood shapes our discernment, or lack thereof: He would have seen my vulnerabilities. He led me to believe that he was sharing custody of two children with his ex-wife. He used to tell me bad things about her, even one story about how she had perforated his ear drum by hitting him with a shoe. I believed what he was saying and didn't realise while we were friends, it was a big lie to cast him in a much different light than he deserved. I admit I got tricked! I still don't know what happened. They—narcissists, sociopaths and any other person whose condition is built on preying on others—are very good at what they do. That's why it's so hard to leave them. I tried to do this unsuccessfully several times and was always pursued until I gave in and returned to the 'family' home. I never gave up wanting to be free of him and the experiences of life with him.

On one occasion, when I tried to divorce him, he came to the hospital I was working at. I was working and was observing the patients who had been admitted for treatment have visits with their family members. I was in the midst of this visit and he walked on the ward and just started shouting and swearing at me. No one stopped him. He was allowed to just come to the hospital and do that without anyone who saw him intervening. After it was over, I told the ward manager and she did nothing about it. The blind eye told him he could engage in this behaviour in public, which he continued to do frequently. He had managed to get me into a position of isolation as is a common occurrence in abusive relationships. I didn't see my family very much. He had so much power and control over me; he could come to work and abuse me whilst I was on duty...uninterrupted. I was vulnerable and felt scared yet I didn't feel empowered to talk with anyone about what had been happening. He even tried to get me fired. He had approached a senior manager demanding that I write an apology to him because of the way I had treated him. He was so angry that he was losing his control of me, he went to great lengths to deconstruct me even more than he had already done.

I remember him throwing me in the bathtub full of water with all my clothes on once. He attacked me and tried to strangle me. I managed to get away and hid upstairs. I lay in bed frozen when I heard him outside in the garden on the phone, screaming to 9-9-9, the police, that I had assaulted him. He had actually punched himself in the face on previous occasion and told his family it was me. When the police came they got me out of bed to arrest me. I broke down and started to cry. They had separated us in different rooms. I think the officers knew what had really happened as they looked at me, a petite woman of only eight stone (112 lbs.) in weight; they encouraged me to talk more as I pleaded with them calmly to let me find child care for my daughter elsewhere before they took me away. I was desperate not to leave her there in the house with him. I tried to be around for all of the children, equally including his own. I'm sure it was hard for them to understand what was happening at the time. I hope that as adults they can know that the things that happened weren't a display of how to have healthy relationships. It's a discussion me and my daughter have had regularly because I wanted her to learn from my experiences and know she is worth much more than being treated this way by anyone.

At the time, the police told me it was the fact that we were both mental health nurses that stopped them from arresting me that night. I was full of emotion and couldn't believe a situation in which I was the real victim could result in me almost getting arrested.

Even at my dad's funeral, he was abusive because I talked to a man! I had been separated from him when my dad had died. We were living in the same house because I didn't have anywhere else to go and I had gone to the solicitors to file for divorce the day before my dad died. I went to stay at my parents' house when my dad's health started to deteriorate the following day. After the funeral, he verbally abused me and my mother, who didn't deserve it especially on that day. It was awful. I felt sick and I knew he was again picking on vulnerabilities now that my dad was no longer around. In his eyes, the "problem" had been my male friend attending my dad's wake and having a drink with me. He waited until he was alone in the house with me and my mother before he verbally and psychologically abused both of us. My dad never liked him and would not have been happy about his behaviour that day, or any other day. My ex-husband used the death of my father to prey on mine and others' vulnerabilities.

One thing I was "allowed" to do when I was married to him, was walk the dogs on my own. I had previously left him before by randomly buying a flat whilst out walking the dog—it was an opportunity I took to try and get away from his abuse. I saw some buildings and went in to enquire about whether the property was for sale. It was indeed for sale, so I managed to get an offer accepted so I could leave his house that we were all living in. I moved there, without anything as he kept all of my personal items, until he pursued me again and I agreed to give it one last go. We bought a house together! The power he had over me meant I felt I had no other choice. Needless to say, it didn't change anything. I'll never forget when I moved into that house, my dad bought me a bottle of champagne and said drink it for the housewarming (with a whisper saying 'or for the divorce'). That bottle turned up after my dad had died and when my divorce finally came through, after a long drawn out period of time that went on longer than the marriage, I enjoyed it as a celebratory drink.

I was a feisty, angry, young woman and he managed to get me in a position where I was afraid. This was his power over me. Sometimes I am still afraid, in a different way than when I lived with him. He stalked me after I eventually left him and managed to stay away from him. I was totally unaware for how long it had been happening. At the time, I was at my new partner's house and we saw a shadow across the window; his car was seen leaving the area, and I called the police immediately because I know the vulnerabilities of being stalked by an abusive ex-partner once you have left them for good. I had no idea it was happening, which is the scary thing.

According to Centers for Disease Control and Prevention (CDC, 2011):

- 7.5 million people are stalked in one year in the United States.
- Over 85% of stalking victims are stalked by someone they know.
- 61% of female victims and 44% of male victims of stalking are stalked by a current or former intimate partner.
- Persons aged 18-24 years experience the highest rate of stalking.
- 11% of stalking victims have been stalked for 5 years or more.
- 46% of stalking victims experience at least one unwanted contact per week.
- This is not dissimilar to the UK where (ONS, 2016):
- On average, 3.3% of women aged 16-24 experienced cyber stalking in 2016/2017 receiving at least one obscene, threatening or unwanted email or social media message within the last year.
- Up to 700,000 women are stalked each year with victims usually only reporting it to the police after the 100th incident.
- The Metropolitan Police Service found that 40% of the victims of domestic homicides had also been stalked.

As if the relationship itself isn't disturbing enough, by these statistics alone, we can gauge that stalkers have a difficult time of letting go—in fact, in some cases, they will kill to maintain control. I find it hard to be in the dark. I don't think he's going to jump out, but the edginess affects me. I feel vulnerable at those times. Now, I am supported by an amazing man whom I'm married to; he showed me what a real relationship could be. This healthy relationship has helped me to grow into who I am today. I still have work to do on myself. I don't think that will ever end, but if what I am left with is the worst of it, then I can live with the residuals of the previous dangerous relationship. I'm not afraid to be me and to live a healthy, happy life. It's this journey that I want to share with you to save you pain or heartache. L.O.V.E Leadership will assist you.

The memories here are vivid and serve as a warning to anyone currently in a dangerous relationship, and the message is for men and women. Please find someone you trust to tell if this is happening to you. Otherwise, you risk getting stuck in a vulnerable position. You have a choice, just as I did. You don't have to let it continue.

I have to tell you that I don't hate this man. I don't hold a grudge and have used the experiences I had with him to make sure that never happened to me again. I've used the experience to help educate my daughter and others. I wish him the best in the future. I don't want him around me and I don't wish him harm. I have forgiven, just not forgotten.

I'm sure this sounds familiar to a lot of people in dangerous relationships—life is happening, a series of events that you can't get a grip on and make significant changes. I'd hoped that he would be civil for a little while after my dad had died. I was disappointed.

Emotional and psychological abuse can be a permanent fixture if you give it power. I can still see the glasses on his face with the lens slightly crooked. He met someone else. He hasn't changed from what I understand, however, this can't be my concern. His problem is with him and he will either work that out or not. He hates himself and tried to find ways to help him deal with that deep self-loathing. That didn't help! It made him more paranoid. He possesses his own story, which he may have yet to deal with.

Here, it is important to note that medical professionals are not immune to substance abuse. For some, it may never impede them from doing their job well, as they are able to compartmentalise areas of their lives masterfully. For others, it is a sure fire to losing their careers and possibly their lives eventually because of the combination of working in a high-pressure, high-risk profession and fusing it with destructive vices. This is something that human beings will consider with alcohol being readily available and a challenge to resist. How many people finish their working day and relax with a large glass of wine or two every night of the week?

## Identifying Detrimental Behaviours

After refusing to give me back my possessions, one day, I came home and all my stuff had been dumped in the back garden of my flat. He had gotten assistance from two of his friends to do this, one who had severe and enduring mental health problems related to substance use. I mention this because I remember getting a call from a community psychiatric nurse one evening saying, “I need to inform you that someone has made threats to kill you. I don’t want you to be worried. He is in hospital now.” The person he spoke about was known to my ex-husband. I was terrified and although my employer offered me the opportunity to meet him after he was released from a secure psychiatric hospital, this never took place. I won’t expand on the detail; however, I learned that he got fixated on me, which I believe was because my ex-husband had been telling him how awful I had been to him.

This was a scary time in my life as a single parent with a young daughter, living alone. I was aware that he knew my address, which worried me. I eventually moved as part of starting my new life, which helped reduce anxieties.

Other things that he had done included phoning some of my friends, telling them he was suicidal and couldn’t live without me. They urged me to go back with him because he regretted how he treated me! Needless to say, I didn’t continue my friendship with them as I needed to prioritise safety for myself and my daughter. I did have some good relationships at that time and this helped to give me the strength that I needed to start building a new life.

I’ve had to recognise and stop the pattern of dating abusive men. It was something problematic that I did from an earlier age and it had showed up in numerous ways. I didn’t go out looking for them; this was an unconscious behaviour at the time. What I recognised through my formal education and interest in people is that I had gotten myself into a *pattern that needed to change.* This pattern came from low self-esteem and a lack of self-confidence, which had developed in my earlier years. It was possible to change. I just needed the awareness and practice to do this to evolve to create a different pattern.

My actions led me to those things that were unpleasant. They didn't just happen to me. People say you make your own luck and it's true—the actions you take, whether conscious or subconscious, impact on you. The more aware you are of yourself and the patterns you follow, the more you can develop, which is where the 'Own' of L.O.V.E Leadership model is important in conducting yourself as a leader and to lead other people. At the time, I didn't have the full awareness of this. I didn't think, *Oh, I know what I'm doing. I'm dating abusive men!* It took me years and years of chipping away and illuminating more information before I realised. It's a steep learning curve.

I want to encourage you to look at yourself and how you end up in situations, especially where you are experiencing repeating patterns of behaviour that you want to change. Look at yourself and think about how you can change and make something different, whether that be a relationship, a feeling or behaviour. I talk to my daughter a lot about liking herself. She's an actor. They take one look at you in that profession and tell you, "No you're not good enough." I'm really keen to make sure that people in that industry get the support they need to thrive. We've seen a large number of death by suicide in the entertainment industry. In fact, as I edit this book, the latest being electronic dance sensation Prodigy's founder and lead, Keith Flint.

As I've said, life experiences will shape you as an adult and this is what needs to be addressed much earlier to minimise the development of poor mental health in an individual or for someone planning and completing their suicide. Reducing stigma is essential as is L.O.V.E Leadership.

## WELLNESS WARRIOR

Kirsten Davenport, Registered Mental Health Nurse and Psychotherapist

Kirsten has worked in the field of mental health for the last twenty-four years, with the last sixteen of those years as a Registered Mental Health Nurse. She works within the inpatient setting and within community teams serving the adult population and young adults in a variety of roles. Because Kirsten's experience spans NHS divisions across the UK with intermittent spells in the private sector, I would call her a wellness warrior through and through. She completed a master's degree in Mindfulness-Based Psychotherapy, which makes her a natural advisor here toward diverse populations.

**Q: What was your start like in the mental health field?**

**A:** On reflection, I feel that I may have chosen to undertake psychotherapy training as I had become increasingly dissatisfied with what I felt I could offer as a Mental Health Nurse to those that I came in contact with. Dissatisfaction with both the systems that I worked within and what I believed was a limited skill set within myself.

I initially started a psychoanalytical training and completed a Post Graduate Diploma, however, it did not offer what I was looking for. Fundamentally I was looking for a way of learning how to come into relationship with another and their experiences in a way which could be deemed supportive.

Having done the training in Mindfulness Psychotherapy, I feel that I have been able to come into relationship in a much more helpful way with not only those that I meet within my role as a Mental Health Nurse but also my colleagues and the systems in which I work.

This leads me onto asking the question, what is it about the *systems* in which we work that makes it difficult to remain in relationship with one another and our service users? It is easy to identify the fundamental causes for some of the challenges that practitioners face, most practitioners would agree that some of the fundamental challenges they face at work are the lack of resources, the time restraints and poor communication with other professionals, all of which is agreed to impact on the quality of care, however moving towards a resolution appears complex. I think mostly as we are working in a time where service demand is constantly on the increase and there appears to be a permanent movement in the system to meet this demand. In order to undertake this challenge effectively there is a requirement for strong leadership and in my experience that is sometimes lacking. This can lead to a fragmentation within the system and clinicians and practitioners feeling confused and disempowered.

When I am able to spend time with the service users, either in a one to one session or as part of a group process, I get back in touch with what the work is about and I guess the 'task'. Fundamentally this is the most gratifying part of my position, working alongside others in their journey and exploration of learning to be able to be with their experience.

One of the advantages for moving from England to Scotland was being able to continue to work for the NHS, something that I value and feel we should attempt to preserve. I have been impressed by some of the service provision and the overall emphasis that is placed on improving the health of the nation and those that access health services. Alongside NICE Guidelines (*https://www.nice.org.uk/*), Scotland makes use of the Psychological Matrix (*https://www.nes.scot.nhs.uk/*), which is a guide to delivering evidence-based psychological interventions and in my experience, routinely referred to.

I have found that there continues to be a diverse provision of support in both mainstream services and the voluntary sector, although this feels tentative and am beginning to observe some of the challenges and pressures that I witnessed in England.

There appears to be recognition of the holistic needs of the health worker also and what is needed in order to support one in continuing to do the work. Training opportunities continue to be available also, which is something that was in demise within English mental health services.

**Q: If you think about Scotland and England and even the United States, are mass violence and suicide rates increasing?**

**A:** I am not sure that there is a significant change in the mass violence that we are witnessing, I wonder if the difference is how it is reported and the numerous streams of media that we can now access that can make it feel overwhelming?

When I consider my own life span, there have been themes of mass violence throughout. I have come to understand this as a process in which what is oppressed 'spills out' because of lack of alternative expression and therefore serves a purpose.

Football hooliganism that was rife in the 70s and 80s I feel offers a good example of where organised violence became a feature during a time of recession and oppression within the UK. I have found the works of Carl Jung and the likes of Joseph Campbell (1955) helpful in coming to think about and understand this territory.

I am particularly interested in the rise that we are seeing in male suicide, a trend that as previously been slowed, but appears to be on the rise again in certain age groups. I find myself wondering if it is related to the movement in society about female empowerment and the changing of the male role within society. In times past, there were clear definitive roles for both genders, and what was expected of them, rightly or wrongly. As part of the societal transformation, I feel males are left with confusion about their role, how to conduct themselves and what it is they can offer. Sexuality and gender are much more fluid and there appears to be an integration of the masculine and the feminine. The process of any psychological integration is acknowledged to be painful and again is widely written about.

I think what is important to recognise is the need for this societal shift whilst equally recognising the huge transformation that will be required within the individual and ensuring there are adequate supports that will require an in-depth understanding.

# Chapter 4

## *Head + Heart = Human*

IN THE UK, THE 'ROYALS' are a prominent news story on a regular basis. Everything the royal family does automatically gets a headline. "Royal Rebel!" "Royal Shock!" "Royal Mystery!"

I, for one, was quite pleased to see another headline and one that will be ever-evolving for a long time, I suspect. I've followed the work of Prince William, the Duke of Cambridge; William's wife, Catherine (Kate), the Duchess of Cambridge, and Prince Harry, His Royal Highness The Duke of Sussex, for some time and watched the positive impact they've had in raising awareness around mental health issues. Megan Markel, Duchess of Sussex, has joined the trio more recently and the good work continues.

At the First Royal Foundation Forum, with the theme "Making a Difference Together," the family discussed their intention to do more work around mental health awareness through their campaign, Heads Together.

In recent interviews, the four have highlighted various aspects of mental health: cause rather than symptoms, addiction, the military and post-traumatic stress disorder (PTSD), and school support in vulnerable, young children.

Prince Harry's personal experience with trauma and its impact on mental health was amplified when his mother, Princess Diana, died in a car accident when he was just 12 years old. He experienced years of anger and panic attacks that were unchecked and subsequently led to him shutting off emotions for the last twenty years.

Subsequently, Prince Harry sought therapy to find relief from his grief and pain. Therefore, he began to address the impact of his tragic loss.

When finally speaking openly to *The Telegraph* in the promotion of Heads Together, Prince Harry said, "People deal with grief in different ways and my way of dealing with it was shutting it out. The ten years that I was in the army, I just dug my head in the sand and it was just white noise. I had to go through a whole period of trying to sort myself out."

During the support I offered to children, young people and families as a volunteer, clinical lead trustee and lead for a bereavement charity over a period of ten years, I have assisted people to understand the grief cycle or my preferred name for it, 'cycle of acceptance'. I've always been involved in supporting people with terminal illness and bereavement as the impact on people's mental health at these times is significant. My father died following a terminal illness and that is where I had to try and understand how I had to manage my own anxiety in order to function on a day-to-day basis. That was almost fifteen years ago now and there isn't a day that goes by where I don't think about him. Milestones and seeing your own children grow up can also magnify the absence of people. It's important to remember to celebrate them at these times.

Prince Harry's decision to open up about his experiences is bold and courageous, given his status, level of exposure and multifaceted obligations. But his goal to help reduce stigma around mental health challenges is the staple of the *Heads Together* initiative partnering with other charities like *Child Bereavement UK*, working to support mental health. This network is tackling stigma, raising awareness, and providing vital help for people with mental health challenges. Therefore, they are supporting mental health and well-being in schools, for youth, for pregnant women and new mothers, and for men in crisis, among others.

Regarding stigma, I want to underscore the Royals' *Mental Health at Work* initiative. Its corresponding website and training tools are designed to equip employees and managers with the aim of creating healthier and more supportive working environments. This is another area of interest for me and one which my company works to promote and address. People can sometimes view a deterioration in mental health as a weakness or a sign of not being able to cope with life or a job. Being able to discuss these things openly and honesty is beneficial in managing and promoting good mental health so it should be encouraged without fear of judgement.

The very inception of this initiative as a high-profile public undertaking speaks volumes. A longstanding question is around the business world's responsibilities and role, if any, in mental health. Why? How? To what end?

I feel so passionately about this subject and have already helped employees and businesses work on changing things to make it a more positive experience within workplaces. I talk a lot about self-awareness and insight. That can sometimes feel a challenge to individuals or companies as it may require them to do something differently. Investing in an improved system that enables time and support to ensure mental health needs are addressed can feel unnecessary. Adaptations of workplace expectations can seem irrelevant whilst people stay focused on the business needs rather than that of the workforce. The message is clear: If we are not taking the time for self-awareness, it's wreaking havoc in our bodies, and that is transferring to teams, corporate entities and society at large.

In corporate and any other organisation, you should enable people to look after their health properly, have good family time, letting them have lunch breaks, but don't pretend you are by listing it in policy and not in practice. Be authentic. Really do it. I expect every employee working within my companies, or any that I'm involved within, to take breaks when they should, not at the beginning or the end of the day because it's not healthy or conducive to good work. They need to take a lunch break. You will get more out of people by supporting their entire lives rather than punishing them, making them feel anxious. I've seen 'warnings' to employees put on a noticeboard declaring, that something is a "disciplinary offence." How is this helpful to a good working environment? Being threatening or creating a culture of fear is not conducive to any working environment—you can challenge people without being threatening. For example, if people want to go see their children in the school assembly, they should not feel worried about asking to go or feel like they need to beg for that time off. It's important to support them to do those things. Organisations would function better and increase productivity if they enabled this type of request more easily. I know it may appear be an inconvenience to a company in that hour, but you'll get a lot more if you consider their individual lives, not just their work hours. People will be happy. Happy teams leads them to be more productive. You gain more by enabling people because they're going to feel content. Sometimes you take care of the small things that have a positive cumulative effect. This is something I promote within my businesses. I have employees who need to respond to the needs of their children above everything else. I never deny this even if it's not always right for me or the business. I just find a way around it to make it work. This is true for any request they make. I've never really been a leader or manager to say no to people's requests regardless of whether they have children or not. However, there are occasions where you may be taken advantage of or flexibility may be unappreciated. This is connected to the human need for boundary setting. These times require you to use your voice and have an open, honest conversation about the struggles. There is usually a compromise to be made that supports everyone's needs. *The key here is to have the conversation.*

I promote honesty as a way of working through this experience and creating a relationship, which is equal and attuned. This requires everyone to take part. It also takes you to feel comfortable with you.

Talk about mental health. Everyone has mental health. Reinforce that mental health and physical health are intertwined. Tell people to look after their mental health. If you break your leg, go to the doctor. If you are having an emotional problem, get help. Talk to your colleagues. I'm not saying drone on and drown people in it. I'm saying make it part of a company culture or a family's way of being. It will take practice as everything else does. It will have a positive effect. I find myself having lots of conversations with people who say 'I've never told anyone that before'. I think this is linked to L.O.V.E Leadership—I'm a good listener, which can feel empowering. It also encourages and engages people to own and voice things for themselves.

It should be okay to talk about things that are important to you. No one should feel judged for expressing how they feel in any given moment. It's helpful to know if someone is struggling with an area in their life. We talked previously about the voice of men and mental health. I often discuss the language used in history that may reduce the likelihood of any male speaking about their truth. For example, have you ever thought about the phrases 'man up', 'be a man about it', 'big boys don't cry' and 'stiff upper lip'. What do they mean to you and how do you think they may be interpreted if we hear them often enough? Are there any other phrases you can think of that may impact on the voice of yourself or another? And why?

Today, I learned from someone I've known for six weeks, that her brother-in-law's wife killed herself over nine years ago. She talked to me quite openly and is still talking from a heartfelt place about what happened. I think she shocked herself in telling me. I got the feeling she probably would not have talked about this with her manager. You can get fearful about it as you don't want people who employ you to judge you. This type of conversation can really help to support someone and requires someone to actively listen. It can also help you.

## Chief People Officers and Other Marvels

Arterne CIC doesn't fit into a box. I try to explain to people what the company does and how it makes a difference, which sometimes leaves them feeling confused. It's about spreading unconditional love. Arterne CIC is based wholly on principles of love: integrity, openness, honesty and enabling people to be the best version of themselves they can be through whatever means of achieving that is possible. For example, if someone turns up on a training course, we're going to try to offer training in a way that will help them get in touch with themselves personally, which has an impact in their life. I'm an advocate for coaching and mentoring for sure. I've had coaches and have gained lots of value from our conversations. The L.O.V.E Leadership Academy supports this notion and is available to everyone by making a simple phone call or sending a message to me. The idea is for groups of people spend time together working through L.O.V.E Leadership in order to help shape their futures. It includes coaching and mentoring. I want it to feel like a life-changing experience to everyone attending, just like it has been for me on my journey.

If you are the leader of a brand or company, there are a few extra things for you to consider in teams and organisations. I will tell you that a few employees won't tell their boss that they are anxious, have low mood, thoughts of suicide, financial troubles, that they might be drinking too much alcohol because they fear the repercussions. They may worry about confiding in a leader, resulting in losing their job. This is why people may need an alternative approach. This doesn't mean someone is a poor leader. I think it's equally challenging for leaders to confide in other senior leaders or peers. There are usually many policies that explain although contrast with: "We're family-friendly and accommodating". And these companies may even have Chief People Officers and other nifty titles on paper and in theory. It's possible that we may get focused on task-orientated priorities and the outcomes desired, which may lose the human element of seeing what's required. Listening to employees without judgement is so important. L.O.V.E Leadership can help individuals and teams to learn, practice and promote these skills.

The reality is, not only do people fear doing something wrong, losing their jobs; they also worry about getting disciplined, having time off or upsetting the boss. People get stuck in these stories. Some of changing this is encouraging ownership and owning your own stuff is never an easy path to take. You might have been brought up despising authority, which gets played out in the relationships people have with managers or leaders. You may feel like you are 'in trouble' which is something only you can address. It's true that sometimes businesses don't make it very easy for people to care for themselves. As a society, we encourage people to work ridiculous hours. We encourage people to be on email all the time. People can't wait anymore. People want instant responses to satisfy their needs. This can have a detrimental effect on health and happiness. Only you can change this for you. The key is to look at all of your options and how you will get there. Create a list of tasks, which tells you everything you need to do isn't going to help you save time or adjust if you don't take action. It's helpful to figure out your destination and how you will get there, which may mean you have to make a decision to stop doing something that is impacting on your life negatively.

You know when you used to send letters? Or make phone calls? There was a cooling off period between tasks. But now, everything is instant. A: "Hey, I sent you an email." B: "Right, I see. Two hours ago. I've literally not sat down to be able to answer your emails". I am someone who used to be working in that way. Now, I don't even have access to my emails on my phone. I may annoy people in some respects because I'm unavailable all of the time. I'm in the field *helping people*, doing whatever I'm doing in the moment. I want to give people my full attention in whatever I'm doing so that I do it well and show them that they are important. I don't want to be distracted with something else—this is a healthy way of being! It can be hard to achieve though. I have used my phone like it's a mini-computer. I've learned to know it's important to know when to switch off. Preparing documents in short notice is usual in my line of work and doing that in the early hours of the morning is not a realistic expectation. Now, we don't live in a perfect world, if it's the norm rather than exception, something is really wrong. Companies have a responsibility to their employees. I've been the employee living the unhealthy lifestyle: being instantly accessible all of the time, having an endless task list, not being enabled to say no. It was me who had to take action to change this.

I would encourage business owners and leaders to seek feedback from employees about what the actual impact of the business demands is on their lives. This includes the senior leaders. And if you are an unhappy employee, choose a life you want to live and head towards it.

The good news is that respected companies like Lyft, Aetna, Unilever and Barclays have recently come out with ground-breaking wellness initiatives. Barclays, for example, rolled out a "This Is Me" campaign, showcasing individual stories of mental health; the campaign started with nine employees and now features more than 200 employees and has been visited over 60,000 times. Others are sending emails reminding staff of using sick days for mental health issues. And the UK government has voraciously promoted the "5 Ways to Mental Wellbeing" for at least a decade (New Economics Foundation, 2008). Those ways, which suggest that even a small improvement in wellbeing can help to decrease some mental health problems and help people to flourish, are:

- Connect
- Be active
- Take notice
- Keep learning
- Give

I spoke as a keynote at the Plymouth Public Health THRIVE Conference in 2017, which focused on Mental Health and these five areas to enable people to consider what would be beneficial to promote good mental health which was well received. Sharing your personal story can have a powerful impact in helping yourself and others, which I have witnessed on many occasions.

## Perfection or Deep Pain?

It cannot be hidden that people do fear the implications of saying 'no'. Having a 'what not to do list' can help people prioritise goals to achieve their desired lifestyle. As I've said before, the L.O.V.E Leadership model includes 'Listen', and quite often while I find that many individuals do listen to individuals, companies may find this more of a challenge, especially when that collective ear from the top may be closed and entirely task focused. When I go into businesses that have reached a point where they need help to function, I usually find cultures of perfection, extreme expectations or limited review processes to obtain an accurate picture. People find it hard to voice their opinion in these cultures because they may get labelled as a "troublemaker." Even if speaking out is for the right reasons. I have been faced with a dilemma in my professional life where I was being told to report inaccurately about waiting times in relation to treatment. This went against my integrity and did not serve people well so I did not collude with this position. The problem remains the same in that organisation, despite many years passing by. The sad thing is the people to suffer the most are the people who are not always getting access to the treatment they need to improve their lives.

As a supporter of individuals and businesses, you will always get honesty, integrity, good intentions, respect, love and openness from me. When I enter a company to set something up or turn something around, I have a voice and I'm not afraid to use it. This is about making improvements for the people in the services being delivered. I've learned how to use this skill effectively. Honest communication is key, and there will be conversations that people will want to avoid. A CEO I work with now laughs at me and says, "I love your style, keep doing what you're doing." Perhaps they do not feel confident to turn things around themselves, or maybe they don't know how to approach communications that may feel uncomfortable. It doesn't matter, we work together to create a good environment for employees and people who use the service equally.

When it comes to workplace culture, open communication is vital to success, according to American Management Association (2019). Consider: "In the absence of open communication, a snowball effect of negative actions can envelop the energy of an organisation. If communication is tentative and secretive, trust—what there is of it—tends to erode. When trust erodes, employees tend to disengage and hold back their thoughts for fear of retribution. They may also begin to feel that management no longer has their best interests in mind, and they may be wary of offering anything over and above the minimal contribution."

As an employee, some habits you form in a workplace are tied to the history of the place and generational imprints in our personal lives. Histories that permit you to behave badly, not in your best interest or that of others. You get people that have better skills in some areas than others, and I think as a corporation, why insist on someone doing a job in a way you want it done if you know they can't do it? They might have other skills that are brilliant, so why not try and pull those out and build on them?

You may be surprised how quickly the tone of an environment can change to be more supportive and compassionate. Leaders can assume a few behaviours that emphasise mental wellbeing among teams and encourage sharing:

- Create and send positive messages that promote great mindfulness and serenity, particularly when employees are in the thick of performing against big deadlines or milestones. Everyone wants to be inspired.
- Make people feel good about themselves by openly recognising the good in people. Ask for the same in return. People will admire your skills and feel inspired.
- Be honest in your communications. Teach people that this isn't about blame. If you need to speak with an individual about their performance avoid doing this in a group setting.

### WELLNESS WARRIOR

Jane Kirby, Registered Manager, Social Worker

Jane is in a unique position in that her social work degree offered a consolidation of her skills and experience, which enabled her to become a more knowledgeable and effective practitioner, managing in the health and social care sector. She has been working in the field for twenty-five years, which gives her a broad view. Here, I wanted to know what she finds urgent and imperative in the next phase of mental health treatment.

**Q: Is everyone vulnerable to mental health issues?**

**A:** I believe that we all experience events/experiences that can cause our equilibrium to become unbalanced. This can lead to mental ill health. Working in my role, you become more aware of methods in which you need to protect and nurture your mental health.

**Q: When it comes to mental health and given the escalating rates of suicide worldwide, what are we not getting as a society and what needs to change?**

**A:** I believe that there is not enough funding for effective services for people experiencing mental ill health, and I think that many people who require mental health services fall through the net, and are not receiving any support. Services that are providing support are not giving the correct level of support for what people need to keep them well and out of crisis. This is not the service's fault, as they are given time allocations and this might not suit some people with more complex mental health needs.

I also think that there is still a huge stigma attached to people with mental health needs. Given the statistics of one in four people experiencing mental health issues, the area is just not given enough discussion/media time. It needs to be higher up the country's agenda. Just today, there was an article on 4 young people who have taken their own lives within 6 weeks of each other. As a nation, there is definitely something we are missing.

I believe that young people today are under a lot of pressure conforming to the media's expectations of 'perfect individuals', 'perfect bodies' etc. Social media has increased these perceptions, and the young people of today are heavily influenced by these unrealistic ideals.

Discussions about mental health needs to start in schools at an early age, and all schools should have a mental health worker, who is able to access services or support if the need arises. This should also include strategies to deal with online bullying. Young people are affected by this, and it can heavily influence them.

# Chapter 5

## *Remembering the Broken Hearts*

I'VE GIVEN YOU LOTS TO think about, so...how do you feel? Thank you for indirectly giving me permission to ask you during the course of this book. Perhaps it's time to take a pause here. #take10

See, it feels soothing, doesn't it?

Looking back, I can see that I've been shaped by all of my experiences. Some have left me feeling anxious and some have left me feeling inadequate. Of course, I wanted to feel better at these times, happier and healthier. I've experienced an internal dialogue that kept me stuck in a pattern of behaviour that didn't enable the best version of me. I was affected by life events such as the death of my father, being in a bad relationship or a job that made me feel unhappy.

These experiences can happen to anyone at any age. The situation almost becomes bigger than the person, "depressing" mood and activities, the person's everyday life. Signs of 'situational depression' may be sadness, feeling nervous, tired and hopeless, changes in sleeping or eating patterns, increased use of alcohol, and physical symptoms such as headaches, digestion issues and heart palpitations.

Note that feeling sad is perfectly healthy and usual. If happiness and joy could be experienced all day long, every day, then there would be a queue of people waiting to buy it! There are decisions and actions you can take to take steps towards this life. Life is a rollercoaster of emotions and all of these feelings that shape who we become. Learning to cope with thoughts and feelings is essential. We can feel sad as a means of empathy toward someone else's situation also; however, it doesn't tend to be all-consuming for everyone like the direct result of our own circumstances.

Situational depression can ease in time as the person is able to make adjustments—and voice what is going on for them in order to get help. Talking about what is going on strongly tends to help improve attitude and perspective, daily behaviours and interpersonal functioning.

Voice is paramount and a fundamental of L.O.V.E Leadership (more in Chapter 9).

Clinical depression, also known as major depression, is characterised by more severe, persistent or chronic symptoms whether a major event occurred or not. To refer to a simple definition, courtesy of National Institute of Mental Health (2018), clinical depression consists of different types:

- persistent depressive disorder (a depressed mood that lasts for at least two years)
- postpartum depression (severe depression experienced by one in seven women after childbirth)
- seasonal affective disorder, or SAD (severe depression triggered by reduced sunlight during winter months)
- and psychotic depression (severe depression triggered by a co-
- occurring psychosis).

The DSM 5 (2019) and ICD 10 (2010) also list similar criteria to meet to be officially diagnosed with clinical depression.

In these cases, the phrases "just get over it" or "stop being lazy and weak" are just insensitive and unrealistic. Circumstances need to be understood. Clinical depression is a medical condition. Severity and frequency of symptoms vary from person to person. According to the National Institute of Mental Health (2016), gender can influence which symptoms an individual with depression experiences. For example, women can experience some specific conditions related to physical and hormonal changes.

Depression is not always visible to outside observers. Symptoms can range from persistent sadness and apathy, in mild cases, to the inability to get out of bed or eat (as Zoe shared in the Foreword of this book) and driving thoughts of suicide, in severe cases.

Three million people in the UK were diagnosed with depression in 2017. Also, according to the WHO, depression will be the second-leading cause of world disability by 2020. Depression affects 25 million American adults each year; just half of them receive treatment. Among those suffering from major depression, up to one in seven will die by suicide. Men are far more likely to die by suicide than women, and people between the ages of 25 and 65 account for half of all recorded deaths by suicide. The Samaritans' strategy 'Working together to reduce suicide 2015-2021' recognises the importance of identifying vulnerable groups of people in order to minimise the risk of suicides occurring.

The Samaritans annual report (2018), focused on UK and Republic of Ireland statistics for suicide, confirmed that there were 6,213 recorded deaths by suicide in 2017, with 392 of those in the Republic of Ireland, overall being a reduced number of deaths. Whereas the statistical data for U.S working age population (person aged 16-64) showed a 34% increase rate of death by suicide between 2000-2016, from 12.9 per 100,000 to 17.3 per 100,000 (U.S Department of Health and Human Services, 2018).

## Fame May Not Be Happiness

In the same week that fashion designer and business woman Katherine "Kate" Spade, aged 55, and Anthony Michael Bourdain, aged 61, American celebrity chef, author and travel documentarian, both connected with New York City, were pronounced dead by means of hanging, I was working in Bristol for a week facilitating a STORM Skills Training for professionals who are on the front lines. Like the celebrity's fans, I was devastated by these back-to-back tragedies as a loss of human life. And like other mental health professionals, I was more determined than ever to educate the masses about depression and its links to suicide—that fame, fortune, family, and even doing what you love are not factors that prevent or reverse it. It's the instilling of hope in a person that will be the most significant and something I have supported people to find on many occasions over the years that I have worked in mental health. However, hope has to be something for individuals to believe in for it to impact positively.

The blow of two beloved genius figures dying by suicide within days of one another struck a chord worldwide. Their careers were quite public, and they had obviously suffered excruciating depressive states and anxiety when the spotlights were not on them. People who knew them intimately spoke of their lifelong battles with depression respectively. It's not clear if either of them ever stated intent to end his or her life. What is clear, is that others knew of their mental health condition. Kate's sister has openly spoken about her belief about Kate's mental illness taking its toll on her. After being found by her housekeeper in her New York City apartment, it's been reported that Kate left her 13-year-old daughter a note, which Kate's husband has spoken out against it being shared publicly. Kate and her husband had been living separately for ten months prior to her death.

When people reach the point of expressing thoughts of suicide, I think others are fearful that if they say anything or ask a question, they are going to make it worse or cause the person to take action. Working as a national consultant for STORM Skills Training, whose training materials directly influence how people, including mental health professionals, are approaching and managing this concerning epidemic. The package is available beyond the UK and provides a consistent framework to discuss what needs to happen when a child, young person or adult mental health has deteriorated and they are expressing thoughts of harming or killing themselves. I have an extensive knowledge of working in this area, but I don't have all the answers.

What I do know is that people are so afraid of getting their response wrong when someone is crying for help it can leave them frozen out of fear. Having "a shoulder to cry on" is not an old-fashioned trend. At the same time, people may avoid someone or a conversation if they don't know how to respond. Over the last couple of years I've seen numerous support groups and agencies pop up all aimed at supporting 'mental health and illness' and whilst I think they are important for the community to be accessing and I support them in their endeavour, I remain committed to the notion of specialist support as quickly as possible for those that need it. For celebrities and busy professionals in particular, their pressures of high art, high life may have contributed to their unpredictable anxiety and/or mood levels or it may have been something that they've always experienced. Regardless, being on the road alone frequently, on top of superhuman demands to juggle various life areas, has been known to intensify symptoms, increase drug and/or alcohol use or interrupt a healthy sleep routine.

Whatever the reason for their lives being stolen and their light being cut from this world that was fortunate to have their contributions, I would like to take a few moments to pay tribute to some that stood out in my own life, and acknowledge their pains, struggles and achievements:

**Tim Bergling 'Avicii', thank you.** A Swedish musician, DJ, remixer and record producer, Avicii was one of the biggest stars of electronic dance music (EDM) in the world, nominated for a Grammy Award in 2013 for "Best Dance Recording" and in 2014, confirmed a collaboration with Madonna via his Instagram account. Other collaborations include Robbie Williams, Wyclef Jean, Chris Martin, Alex Ebert and Coca-Cola. Tim was only 28 when he died through blood loss due to self-inflicted injuries made by a broken wine bottle in April 2018. Tim's mother was an actress. Tim was one of four children and was inspired by his brother to begin mixing at aged 8. At the age of 16, he began posting his remixes on electronic music forums which led him to his first record deal. He continued producing music albums and touring until he retired in 2016, long suffering stress and poor mental health. In 2017, he released a six-track EP saying, "I'm really excited to be back with music once again," and announced a documentary called *Avicii: True Stories.* At the time of his death in 2018, he had over 200 unreleased songs and more in development. Following the release of his single "SOS" in April 2019, the album, *Tim*, will be released in June 2019. This album is his work leading up to his death and all proceeds from sales will go towards the *Tim Bergling Foundation.*

**Chester Charles Bennington, thank you.** An American singer, songwriter, musician and actor who was more recently known as the lead vocalist in Linkin Park died by hanging in July 2017, aged 41, after a long battle with substance use issues and depression. Known as one of the top rock musicians of the 2000s, with the "Hybrid Theory—Crawling" being recognised as the most literal song lyrically ever written by Chester (and one of my favourite songs). As one of four children, his mother was a nurse and his father was a police detective who investigated child sex crime. Sadly, Chester was a victim of sexual abuse for many years by an older male friend. He was aged 7 when it started and it continued until he was 13. He was too afraid to speak out about it happening for fear of not being believed. This experience, alongside being bullied at school, impressed upon his life journey significantly. In memory of Chester, his wife, Talinda, has gone on to do some amazing work, becoming an advocate for speaking up about mental health, setting up 320 Changes Direction to tackle mental health and addition head on, saying that "it's nobody's fault, it's years of untreated mental health." Their son has recently joined the movement to help promote this important notion. *#fuckdepression #makechesterproud*

**Anthony Michael Bourdain, thank you.** An American celebrity chef, author and travel documentarian, born the eldest of two sons to his mother who was Jewish and his father who was Catholic, was not raised in a specific religion. After marrying his childhood sweetheart, they divorced in 2005 after the strain of working away from home took its toll. Anthony had been working on his brilliant CNN series, *Anthony Bourdain: Parts Unknown* when he died in June 2018. Anthony was best known for his culinary writings, television presentations and books on food, cooking and travel adventures.

**Kurt Donald Cobain, thank you.** An American singer, songwriter and musician, best known as the guitarist and front man of the rock band Nirvana, found success with "Smells Like Teen Spirit" from their second album *Nevermind*, in 1991 (still one of my favourite songs). Kurt, the son of a waitress and automotive mechanic, experienced their divorce when he was 9 years old and was noted to have later said it had a profound impact upon his life. He also witnessed the domestic violence towards his mother when she started a new relationship. Kurt bullied a boy at school and was also bullied; he pretended to be gay and was considered a "teenage rebel." As a result, his father took him to therapy. Kurt suffered addiction, health problems and depression and died by gunshot, at the age of 27, in April 1994, a few weeks after an incident in which he was visited by the police in Seattle, where they confiscated several guns and pills. Kurt had reported that he wasn't suicidal at this point. It's known that Kurt experienced the personal and professional pressures of fame and expressed, "I'd rather be hated for who I am, than loved for who I am not." Kurt is remembered as one of the most iconic and influential rock musicians in the history of alternative music. In 2005, a sign was put up in Kurt's hometown in Washington, as a tribute, which says, "Welcome to Aberdeen—Come As You Are."

**Keith Charles Flint, thank you.** An English vocalist, dancer and motorcycle racer, founded electronic dance act, the Prodigy, whose seven of eight albums reached No. 1 in the UK. Born to parents Clive, engineering consultant and Yvonne, who separated when Keith was young. Keith was unhappy and feuded with his parents, was disruptive in class and expelled from school at age 15. Keith worked as a roofer and later embraced the acid house scene. His new punk look in the "Firestarter" video saw him as the front man of Prodigy. He was 49 when he died by hanging in March 2019. Keith had previously purchased and renovated the Leather Bottle pub in Pleshey, Essex, where he became a popular landlord.

**Lucy Gordon, thank you.** An English model who became the face of Cover Girl in 1997 before pursuing a career in acting. Born in Oxford to parents Richard and Susan, she lived in New York for several years before moving to Paris. Appearing alongside Heath Legder in *The*

*Four Feathers*, 2002, she also played the reporter *Jennifer Dugan* in the 2007 film *Spider-Man 3.* Lucy died in her Paris home by hanging, aged 28, shortly before her 29th birthday in May 2009. It has been alleged that this followed an argument with her boyfriend who was asleep in the flat at the time of her death. Lucy had just made a dramatic breakthrough in her career with *La Vie Heroique*, playing the role of *Jane Birkin.*

**Michael Kelland John Hutchence, thank you.** An Australian musician, singer-songwriter, actor, co-founder, lead singer and lyricist of the rock band INXS, died by hanging, aged 37, in November 1997. Born to parents, Kelland, businessman, and Patricia, make-up artist. Michael's parents separated when he was 15 years old. He rose to fame through his music and won seven awards at the 1984 Countdown Music and Video Awards ceremony. Michael is known to have struggled with depression following an assault that left him with a head injury and substance use issues.

**Heath Andrew Legder, thank you.** An Australian actor and music video director, Heath graced our screens in nineteen films, including, "10 Things I Hate About You," "A Knight's Tale," "Monster's Ball," and "Brokeback Mountain" for which he was awarded New York Film Critics Circle Best Actor in 2005 for his portrayal of Ennis Del Mar. He also received a Golden Globe nomination for Best Actor in a Drama and an Academy Award for Best Actor. Heath died in January 2008, aged 28, by what was considered to be an accidental intoxication from prescription drugs. He had suffered insomnia for some time. Heath had finished his last performance a few months earlier as The Joker in "The Dark Knight." Heath's parents, Sally, a French teacher and Kim, a racing car driver and mining engineer, separated when he was 10 years old, divorcing when he was 11. Heath appeared in "Home and Away" one of Australia's most successful television shows in 1997. He has been referred to as one of the best actors of his generation.

**Lee "Alexander" McQueen, thank you.** Sensational British fashion designer and couturier, who worked as chief designer for

Givenchy from 1996-2001 and founded his own Alexander McQueen label in 1992. His achievements earned him four British Designer of the Year awards as well as the Council of Fashion Designers of America, Inc (CDFA), International Designer of the Year and a CBE in 2003. Lee Alexander had publicly spoken about his realisation of his sexual orientation at age 6, the rocky period to acceptance that followed after telling his family he was gay at aged 18, his struggle with addiction, anxiety and depression for many years. Lee Alexander had missed psychiatric sessions and taken overdoses on previous occasions. It's reported that he overdosed immediately prior to his death by hanging in February 2010, aged 40, just days before London Fashion Week, the night before his mother's funeral. Lee Alexander touched the lives of so many people and it was only last year that I attended Port Eliot Festival, Cornwall, UK and listened to his influence and renowned reputation for pushing the boundaries of fashion.

**Norma Jeane Mortenson 'Marilyn Monroe', thank you.** An American actress, model and singer in the 1950s known for playing "blonde bombshell" characters and the emblematic attitude for the era meant she became a sex symbol. She died prematurely in August 1962, aged 36, through an overdose, after a lifelong struggle with anxiety, depression and problematic substance use. Born in Los Angeles, to Gladys, who was considered mentally and financially unprepared for motherhood, her father was unknown, Norma used her mother's maiden name "Munroe" in later life. Norma's early childhood was stable and happy. Norma was placed with foster parents where Gladys lived with them and travelled to work until forced to move back to her hometown and only visiting her daughter on weekends. The contact between them rarely occurred again after Gladys suffered a "mental breakdown" and was diagnosed with paranoid schizophrenia, spending the rest of her life in and out of hospitals. Becoming "ward of the state," Norma was brought up by family connections, foster parents, foster homes and in an orphanage. Norma was sexually abused, shy, withdrawn and developed a stutter. At 16, she married James "Jim" Dougherty, aged 21, who was a factory worker and the neighbour's son. Her husband joined the Merchant Marine and Norma pursued a career in modelling when her husband was shipped to the Pacific. By 1953, she was featured as the centre-fold for the first issue of *Playboy.* Inadequate pay and poor contracting led her to become a founder of her own film production company, Marilyn Munroe Productions. The most famous scene of Marilyn was one that gathered 2,000 spectators as she posed for the film photo shoot “The Seven Year Itch” on a subway grate causing her skirt to blow up, a fantastic publicity stunt that created pictures still popular today.

**Kate Noel Spade, thank you.** An American fashion designer and business woman who created Kate Spade New York, which now has more than 140 retail shops and outlet stores across the U.S. and more than 175 shops internationally. The new brand, Frances Valentine, launched in 2016 continued after Kate's death in June 2018, promoting the Love Katy collection of designs in honour of Kate.

**Gary Andrew Speed, thank you.** Professional footballer and manager from Wales, played for Leeds United youth team, Leeds United, Everton, Newcastle United, Bolton Wanderers and Sheffield United. He captained the Wales national football team up until he retired from international football in 2004, as the most capped outfield player for Wales. In 2010, Gary was appointed manager of Sheffield United, leaving to manage the Wales national team a few months later. Gary's family were all from Chester. Gary, reportedly described by his mother as a “glass half empty person,” had texted his wife four days before his death about the possibility of suicide and then ruled it out as he looked to his future with his wife and their children. Gary had not formally spoken about any possible mental health issues before his wife found him hanging in their garage, in November 2011, aged 42. After his death, the conviction of Gary's coach revealed information from an anonymous witness who said they had seen Gary being abused by the former coach, although this had been denied by Gary when interviewed at the time of the allegation against the former coach. Gary's widow's story is captured in the book *Unspoken* released in September 2018, which describes the aftermath of the tragedy and her road to recovery. All proceeds from the book go to Heads Together Charity, tackling mental health issues.

**Robin McLaurin Williams, thank you.** An American actor and comedian born in Chicago, to parents Laurie, former model, and Robert, senior executive in Ford Motor Company's Lincoln-Mercury Division, began his career performing stand-up comedy in San Francisco and Los Angeles, rising to fame playing an alien in the sitcom "Mork & Mindy." The iconic actor and comedian was known for his improvisation skills and has been called the funniest person of all time. Robin had fallen foul to addiction early on, he suffered from severe depression, heart problems and had been long suffering of Lewy body dementia "disease" before his death by hanging, aged 63, in August 2014. Robin was a well-known philanthropist, made benefit appearances to support literacy and women's rights, as well as veterans, travelling thirteen countries to perform to over 100,000 troops. There is so much more that this wonderful man did and there have been so many tributes paid to his lifelong contributions to the world. (He was one of my daughter's favourites). The lights of Broadway were darkened for the evening of 14th August 2014, shortly after his death, in honour of his theatre work.

What we see here is every country, every generation and every decade affected by mental health, life experiences, thoughts, feelings, behaviours and the need to share this freely to get support in order to heal as best you can. Hopelessness is still the biggest single indicator of suicidal behaviour, which I believe can be altered through the sharing of L.O.V.E Leadership. That's why I pledge to continue to have a positive impact upon the life of those people in the spotlight as well as those who are not, through offering support, a confidential conversation, a listening ear, help with ownership, speaking up, making change, education, open communications and empowerment.

## Modern Pressures Affect Everyone

News of someone dying by suicide is a tragedy whether the person is known to you personally or not. My work within children and young people's mental health services has meant that I have become aware of people under the age of 18 who have died by suicide, which is something that will never get easier. In order to increase understanding of suicide by different occupational groups in the U.S, the Centers for Disease Control and Prevention analysed seventeen States suicide rates for ages 16-64 (working age). The male group with the highest death rate by suicide was Construction and Extraction, which showed a staggering 53.2 per 100,000. This reflected England's findings for men which identified low-skilled labourers in construction in the highest vulnerability groups (Office National Statistics, 2017). However, female death by suicide rates in the U.S. were identified as being from Arts, Design, Entertainment, Sports and Media. Of interest, this same group for men, from 2012-2015, were shown to have the largest increase of death by suicide (U.S. Department of Health and Human Services, 2018).

The recorded death by suicide rate has fallen significantly overall in the UK since 2007, with male suicide rate being the lowest it has been in 30 years, it has been evidenced that middle aged men (aged 45-59 years) have seen a considerable rise in death by suicide from 18.3 per 100,000 to 25.1 per 100,000 in 2013. In 2017, statistics confirmed that men were three times more likely to take their own lives than women and in the Republic of Ireland men are four times more likely to take their own life than women. Key facts revealed in 2018, showed men aged 45-49 as the group with the highest rate of suicide in England, men aged 40-44 in Wales, men aged 45-54 in Scotland, men aged 35-39 in Northern Ireland and men aged 25-34 in the Republic of Ireland. Although it's important to remember that the suicide rate overall for UK men had decreased by 3.1% and women 2% between 2016 and 2017, decreased 11.8% for men in the Republic of Ireland and women 9.1%, increased 4.5% for men in Wales and 45% for women, decreased 1% for men in Scotland and increased 24.3 % for women.

People aren't always getting the psychiatric care early on in the UK as the NHS faces pressures and has referral criteria thresholds that mean people need to be severely unwell before they get help. There is stigma to tackle within medical personnel and other health care professionals who not only have the pressure to succeed and take care of other people's lives, if they admit illness, they feel they have to worry about their certifications and credentials for the jobs in which they are employed. However, we all have mental health and therefore, have the potential to experience mental ill health regardless of who you are or what you do for a living. We can reduce stigma through more open communications, enabling people to feel that they can speak freely without fear of judgement and make getting help a priority, rather than being considered a weakness.

I've spoken at conferences and worked with children and young people about reducing stigma around the mental health term. I feel passionately about that and therefore, take a stand to inform people about the following: No. 1, you have mental health. Everyone has mental health. No. 2, talking about it is connective. And No. 3, mental health and physical health are linked.

I suggest everyone read Nicola Morgan's book, *Blame My Brain.* The book is written for young people, although the book also offers a lot of information and clarity for adults, especially if they are struggling with teenagers and don't feel that they can understand them, I suggest they get the book, read it and then pass it on to that young person to read because it sparks everyone to think about their situation. Most people that buy the book and read it tell me how brilliant they think it is it is. The message is simple. It considers baby brain development, teenage brain development and much more. It includes a fun quiz in which you choose the *feeling* by looking at photographs of people's eyes only, which is very interesting. Adults have the ability to read facial expressions more easily whereas, young people aren't always able to interpret what they see. Did you know that? I continue to work across all age ranges, even from as early as in pregnancy. Why don't we talk about baby brain development? Teenage brain development? How your personality develops and what affects it? All of this information helps us to know what shapes our evolution. And I always say, "It's not the experience you have that shapes you. It's what you do with it". You can build resilience at any age, which helps to balance the risks people face and the ability to bounce back from those risks. Protective factors are important in managing risks and building resilience for better life outcomes.

For many years, I've worked to instil a mental health curriculum in the school system. It's something that often gets overlooked or dismissed as the responsibility of another service. I've developed a complete skills-based training package and spoken to a local school about developing an accredited qualification focused on mental health for young people. Confidence and self-worth, whether you like yourself, whether you think other people like you all play such a part in role in emotional identity and development. This isn't just limited to young people either. It's something that many adults continue to struggle with regardless of age. People are so private and worry about saying things out loud for fear of being judged or looking foolish when it comes to mental health or personal circumstances. But everything's brilliant on Facebook, right? A big party.... A social media party, where it's either high party or high tragedy, from bar mitzvahs to selfies in hospital beds! Maybe it's worth determining why we are private other than against a social media wall, a veneer. Is privacy a way to mask pain? Is there something about attracting support through sympathy or is it easier to share some information to avoid having to share the whole truth? It's hard to determine what is real and what is not sometimes. Does that really matter if it's about someone else's choice for life? And do we really need to compare ourselves with others? Could we be well-intentioned in every interaction we have with someone? Do we feel blamed or criticised? Who are we being when we are thinking these things? Could we learn how to engage with healthy challenge and discussion with people rather than about people?

These are all considerations within every aspect of the L.O.V.E Leadership model.

You now know that at the age of 25, I married someone 13 years older than me and that he didn't treat me well. I promised myself I would never experience that ever again—processing and hard work on me to find who I was again and not live hyper vigilantly from a place of fear. It was important to me to educate and be a good role model for my daughter and never wanted her to experience what I had within the relationship, as well as some of those prior to my marriage. Even with my sister, Lucy, who has looked up to me as a role model for change, I've reassured her that I had to also find my way to be that role model. Some of her decisions still lead her down the path I was in, a place of silence and isolation. She has tools though. She has me to talk to and I will always be there for her even when we disagree. Difference in opinion or framework can create some of the best conversations for starting or continuing a journey.

Men may be less apt to admit they need help, and this is widely discussed within society. My companies encourage the voice of men and mental health frequently and love to support other community groups. As such, I met with a man who had been doing similar things because his rugby club experienced the aftermath of three suicides in the last three years. All were men in their forties and belonged to their community through playing rugby or bringing their children to play rugby. He is passionate about ensuring that everyone has someone to talk to and wants to try to prevent anyone else from dying by suicide by them believing that help is out there for them. When we spoke, he said he wants to ensure that everyone has someone to talk to and wants to provide opportunities for men to talk. All of the deaths were unexpected, which made it so shocking for people to hear or comprehend. People are still trying to come to terms with what happened. What is fantastic is something so tragic is generating something good. This caring man is trying to get people to talk about mental health and the club has formed its own charity in support of this aim for which they raise funds. We talked about the stigma surrounding the mental health term, particularly for men, and he has experienced stigma. Given my experience speaking nationally about reducing stigma and supporting young people, he wanted to know if I had ideas that could help him. He wasn't outwardly overwhelmed with emotion, but I could sense him holding it in and focusing on the practical aspects of how he could support the community. We were at a business meeting and we had only met for the first time. I could see the emotion rise when he spoke; these men were his friends, and he couldn't make sense of it.

I didn't really know the circumstances of the three men we spoke about, I do know there were things that he mentioned that are considered risk factors when people have low mood or depression. A lack of self-confidence may have been at play, along with a lack of presenting their true selves at times? Something is happening inwardly; however, many people are presenting something else outwardly. The internal dialogue happening can keep people in a pattern of behaviour that may not be having a healthy impact upon them or their life choices. They're not being honest with themselves or aware of what's happening, which is creating a tension and conflict within. They may be afraid of feeling vulnerability. The pressure of always having to be strong, right, clever, the best does get under your skin eventually.

Does any of this speak to you?

## Addiction—We Need to Talk Openly About This, Too

In my experience there is an equal challenge, or it can seem harder, for people with drug and alcohol addiction to ask for help because there is quite a lot of judgment and stigma in this area, too. I've heard people say, "Well, they choose to do it, they can choose not to." And I would say that there is an element of choice to continue to use substances; however, there is equally an element of distorted coping going on and physical or psychological reliance. In one of the projects I set up in 2015, now led within one of my companies, Operation Snow and the addition in 2017, Operation Snow *#notjustforchristmas,* it used the generosity of Christmas time to spread unconditional love and Christmas spirit all throughout the year. It was set up to provide somewhere for people to spend Christmas Day together with warmth, love, food, laughter and good conversation if you want it. It's about reducing barriers and the "them and us" power imbalance where people feel they are giving up something to help less fortunate on Christmas Day and through the year. This is not the position of Operation Snow as we strive to create a dynamic that promotes equality by understanding and accepting difference without judgement. We encourage people on their own, low-income families and those who are homeless to come along and spend time with us. We also offer essential items to people who need them all throughout the year and help to connect them up with other services who offer longer-term help or accommodation when needed. The truth is that it doesn't matters who people are within Operation Snow because it's about being together on Christmas Day and then making sure everyone has what they need to survive during the year. On some occasions, when talking about resources for homeless people, people have offered to donate money to help provide things Operation Snow needed, although they made it very clear that they didn't want to spend their money on helping "addicts." They wanted it spent on "families and older people only." This is disappointing to hear as I believe that everyone should be able to access help regardless of which "group" they are deemed to fit into.

Even if mental illness sets in prior to any substance use, these people are more likely to get segregated from the mainstream as *bad and useless* because they can no longer physically stop abusing the drug without proper care and even then, a lifelong challenge. Often, it can take numerous attempts to actually achieve being drug- or alcohol-free, or make any progress towards their goal. It also takes strength to maintain a position of abstinence.

I relay my message to the general population in a simple way to try and help people make sense of the power of any addiction or desire by asking: What is your favourite dessert? Cake? Ice cream? How many times have you tried to give it up and then gone back to that cake or ice cream? It's not that easy, is it? I don't have to tell you that sugar is an addiction, too. It may not hinder your job or get you thrown on the street, but that addiction is taking its toll on your body, ability to focus, energy level, and possibly more. The "Sugar Smart" campaign (2019) aims to address this taking a "harm reduction" approach. We could even talk about coffee consumption here or the after-work glass of wine. Human beings look for things that increase pleasure in life and habit-forming behaviours can impact negatively. Something to reflect upon for certain, as who we are determines the choices we make and therefore, life outcomes.

There have often been times where I've been talking to my daughter and she has said she was struggling with her confidence. It's hard being a woman, being young and growing up—even if your mother is a mental health nurse. It's part of developing in the world we live in, especially in her area of interest, creating art, performing and entertainment. We were talking about self-esteem and not letting the challenges of early adulthood, including the definition of success in art, entice her to drink more than the usual glass of wine at dinner or responsibly during social occasions. She pointed out that I instilled self-acceptance and speaking her mind, self-respect, and that she had no reason to turn to drug or alcohol use as a means of coping.

Young people may take risks and experiment as they transition into adulthood, which is widely known, for some it passes by and for others it becomes much more problematic as they search for something to sooth them. I think open conversation has helped with her choices, although she hasn't confided everything in me as I continue to find out over time! It's true, teenagers have secrets!

I encourage people to acknowledge their lack of confidence with themselves and others where possible. It's important to ask yourself why you're feeling less capable or vulnerable. What's affecting your confidence levels? Do you need more training, more experience? Or is your feeling actually hesitation or intuition that it may not be the right person, time or situation and has nothing to do with confidence? It's good to be curious about what is going on for you in any given moment and consciously address something, which starts from within.

Consider '*why is self-esteem important?*' The lower your self-esteem is, the easier it is to get into challenging or unhealthy relationships or into a work atmosphere or dynamic that is insidious. Perhaps you become a "people pleaser" or lose your identity or sense of belonging. Some parents have an eagerness to encourage their children to "get into sports, do better in class, get qualified and do extra studies or have a well-paid job and become rich" whereas, others won't see those as significant achievements. Regardless, we have to consider, '*Are they focusing their encouragement on the needs of their children or is something else happening here?*'

Some people think that success is measured by having money, or things like the best job, the best job title, the most expensive car or the biggest house. They strive for the things in which they compare themselves with other people when in reality, success could be having a good relationship with other people, doing things for yourself and living the life you want to live, or be as simple as meeting up with your friends and making good choices for yourself.

I'm curious about people who don't have their own definition of success and judge themselves against what they deem is the success of others. If they are trying to mirror others' terms of prosperity and fulfilment without being introspective and pausing to feel around inside, they may become an empty shell. Living up to what is expected of you can also take its toll. I meet lots of people who are striving for "better" and this may not always be based on their desires, it could be what they think others will think of them in achieving such perceived "greatness." These are the people who may lose a lot of time in discontent and disjointedness. They may become unhappy, have low mood and become clinically depressed or suicidal as they pressure themselves for something which may not be what they want deep down. It's key to consider how you determine happiness and what you need to do for yourself to create the life you want. It's true where our attention goes, growth flows.

## One Jump to Hope

When addressing the topic of suicide prevention in training or presentations, I often cite the story of Kevin Hines, whose suicide attempt was the catalyst for being an activist and advocate for mental health treatment. Kevin has a powerful message to those who feel hopeless and like they have nowhere else to turn, which is informed by his own personal experiences. It is thought provoking and high in emotion. He is one of only thirty-six people to survive the fall from the Golden Gate Bridge. The story promotes that even on the edge of life, there can be happy endings, too! #beheretomorrow

Kevin took a bus ride to the Golden Gate Bridge in September of 2000. Kevin had woken that morning with low mood and thoughts that wouldn't shift, "Jump now," said the voice in Kevin's head. "And

I did. I was compelled to die." Kevin leaped over a rail and began a free fall that would reach 75 miles per hour on impact. The moment his fingers left the railing, he felt instant regret.

"I thought it was too late, I said to myself, '*What have I done, I don't want to die*'," says Hines, 36. "I realised I made the greatest mistake of my life. I thought I had to die and I was wrong."

Hines fell about 240 feet in just four seconds. He crashed feet first into the waters below, crushing spinal vertebrae and breaking an ankle. But he survived. Many factors contributed to Kevin's miraculous survival, including a sea lion that kept him afloat until he could be rescued by the Coast Guard.

Now, Hines travels the world to speak about suicide prevention and mental health, telling his story to share hope and to help others stay alive. Self-education and helping people to grow by sharing your knowledge with others is very rewarding.

## WELLNESS WARRIOR

**Dr. Gill Green, Chief Executive Officer, STORM Skills Training CIC**

It was whilst she was working with children who had learning disabilities that Gill Green first thought about a career in nursing. However, during her training in this field, she became aware of a number of people who also had mental health problems, but who were not receiving the care that they needed. Soon after qualifying, she retrained as a dual qualified mental health nurse with the intention of returning to learning disability services. Fate took her down a different route and she remained working in mental health, eventually becoming a sister working on an acute ward and in the community. During this time, she completed the first of her degrees part-time, a BA (honours) in Social Studies that helped to provide a social and philosophical perspective to her clinical experience of mental illness.

Many patients Gill supported often expressed that life was so hopeless for them that they thought about ending their life. Gill, like many others, felt ill-equipped to respond to and effectively support the people she was trying to help. A chance job advertisement in a national paper for a trainer and researcher on a university study brought Gill and STORM® together in 1997. The 12-month project was an opportunity to learn new skills to take back to clinical practice. Fate, too, played a hand in what happened next. Professor Linda Gask interviewed Gill for the job, the first meeting of what would eventuate into a long and successful partnership: the meeting of the founders of STORM Skills Training CIC.

Here, Gill answers a few questions about the suicide prevention-training model that has turned into an independent and global social business that is having a positive impact, not only in suicide prevention, but also around social change for mental well-being.

**Q: It blows my mind that some people still separate physical health from mental health. Connect the dots, would you?**

**A:** STORM is all about suicide prevention. With that, it comes from my experience and my cofounders' experience in mental health, and trying to understand someone's story and thinking about the person and just not suicide in itself. Years ago, things were very different, and we've got a long way to go, but twenty years ago, we were working in mental health services and found a lot lacking in terms of how we help someone thinking about suicide. That is how STORM evolved from literally our own personal experiences; Linda fore-fronted the organisation, along with a colleague then I came on. From a clinical point of view, my experience was the same. I wanted to help people with suicidal thoughts. Quite miraculously and metrically, we've developed something that seems to be useful. We didn't set out to have a social enterprise that would self-generate income so we could continue to do our work and add value. We wanted something that was useful, but our thoughts were that it would just be another research project for positive changes from the training we would develop then be put on the shelf like everything else. We hit on something that we felt was needed—skills-based training. From there it generated interest from National Health Service and word of mouth. It evolved within the University of Manchester as a not-for-profit venture where we were generating income through the trusts and other organisations. We did that quite successfully and developed the project further and extended our network. It escalated to the point where we're in Australia now. Then the university decided we needed to do something around a business model rather than it stay within the university.

Being a clinician and then an academic, I was frightened about stepping into an entrepreneurial role. We wanted to hold true to our philosophy that no one should profit from another person's distress. We didn't want to go down the non-governmental organisation (NGO) route either. In the UK, they created a legal model called a Community Interest Company. That was to ensure that a social enterprise was true to its word, asset lot, whereby we pay good wages, pay taxes then everything else is poured into the social enterprise to develop the product further and add value to community engagement programs. Again, research project to social enterprise model, which fit us. The value is in the product to help frontline staff develop the skills to help vulnerable people thinking about suicide. Our extra stuff is that we hold seminars and conferences and help other organisations with their conferences. They are free to attend. In the UK, the NHS can't afford to send their staff on seminars, conferences. They are massively oversubscribed! We get people from immigration services, social care, NGOs, who have the benefit of people coming to conferences speaking about their work.

We also have the "Hey! Are you okay?" campaign. That is to help us understand distress before anyone becomes suicidal. Training people to understand how to recognise anyone who becomes suicidal is too late. We can help each other and ourselves alleviate distress before suicidal thinking occurs. That is when we know we're doing the right thing.

**Q: Looking back on your own life as a teenager grappling with homophobia, do you find that the lesbian, gay, bisexual, transgender (LGBT) population is still more susceptible in the UK?**

**A:** That is a very good question. We've shifted to a more open, accepting society in that we have hate crime laws. We also have gay marriage. Things have changed dramatically. I wish I was 16 again and coming out because it would be far different and much better. I'm happy to be part of history and making changes within that time because I was out. Fortunately, I didn't have experiences where I was beaten up or anything, but I may have experienced covert discrimination where I would have gotten a job if I were straight. My whole journey has led me to here though so I can't say I'm upset about that. If you ask the younger people in 10 or 20 years about their experiences, it will be a better time. "Tolerant" now is that I'm still guarded about my personal safety, and my wife's, and find it hard to walk down the street holding hands. I was reading an article the other day about a young person who got beaten up for walking down the street holding hands with her partner. How far have we come? In terms of health, it's about your own acceptance of yourself. That is never going to change. It's down to the individual growing up in a home that may have prejudice or that has not switched onto gayness. Gay kids grow up in a straight world so they have to understand who they are and how they can be themselves in a straight world. A graduate worked for us a couple of years back; some time into employment she told us she was gay and we said, we know anyway! She said she still struggles even though people knew: How do I deal in this straight world? We still have to be mindful of that even though we live in a tolerant society.

**Q: Back to mental health in general, where does drug addiction come in and how are people trained to handle this multipronged face to not wanting to live?**

**A:** It's so complex. If you go back and not pick drug addiction and pick alcohol, that in itself can perpetuate the troubles that someone has and their thinking around suicide. People are very complex. We can't pick out any one particular thing. It's not to say it does not have a feature, but there are other things there as well. Because of that disinhibiting and the nature of alcohol to do that and impulsivity, these are the two biggest things that would turn thoughts to actual action. What we need to understand is people's distress and someone's ability to cope and when they can't cope anymore.

You do need empathy in this space; it's not something easily taught or easily learned. You need the ability to consider what it's like in someone else's shoes. You have to naturally think about other people, their predicaments, their problems, and how to help them help themselves. Cindy fits well within our philosophy and we fit well with hers. She's a hell of an empathetic person.

**Q: What are your long-term plans?**

**A:** For STORM, I am humble to think we're still here after so long and doing well. I'm building remarkable relationships locally and want to increase activities in the community. Personally, I'm quite shocked to say I'm an entrepreneur. I'm learning a lot from this role and being a leader. I'm blessed with the team that I've got. I can learn from them. What I would like to do is consider setting up one or two social enterprises. What has become clear is that we talk about mental health and how it impacts the workplace. There is a general movement toward employers to create awareness with employees around staff's emotional wellbeing. We're not there yet. It's almost like a checkbox exercise still. This is where the "Hey, are you okay?" Campaign comes in. If we can engage companies with this campaign, it will change the culture within the company to accept that people could be performing better if they're able to say they're not coping very well so they can deal with it. This is our culture within our organisation. For instance, I had cancer at the beginning of the year and my team just stepped up. They were just incredible. If I didn't have an educated team, things would not get done and naturally die. It's a positive in the workplace when we understand when people are not feeling great and we can get them through those times. Their performance is better, the bottom line is better. It helps us think of how we can engage with people outside of the workplace, like our friends and families. I want to generate that cultural change. Then we have a chance to think about how we do business. It's too heavy on making profit and not enough wellbeing. If I can change that by setting up a social enterprise or two, that would ultimately be good.

# Chapter 6

## *Sacred Systems, Brilliant Solutions*

LET'S BE HONEST. AS CHILDREN, we're not educated about how to have good relationships or how to live our lives in general. This is not taught in school. Our education system is broken. If you think about it, what's changed in the last thirty years? And it's something reiterated by my daughter when we discuss her mainstream educational experience. Practical things like how to rent or buy a property and how you keep up with a mortgage? And what happens if you don't? It's all academic, isn't it? Wouldn't an education of life itself be useful alongside the achievement of 5 GCSEs Grade A-C? In England, there has been more emphasis on mental health in schools and a demonstration that actively looking after mental health can have a positive impact on academic achievements.

Platform 50, a women's coaching and mentoring project, for ages 16-25, which I set up initially in 2017 and is now led by one of my companies, supports women with a number of challenges including anxiety, exam stress, educational issues and behaviours, bullying, bereavement, experience of terminal illness, mental health problems, relationship issues, family life pressures, low mood and depression, suicidal thoughts, financial worries and work pressures. It is individualised support and the young person can decide what help they need, then meet and chat regularly with a Platform 50 coach and mentor to help work things out. I know of a young person being supported right now who, based on her words, would not have made it through her education if it hadn't been for the support of Platform 50. She was on the verge of being asked to leave her educational institute because of legitimate poor attendance, due to her personal situation. The magic of Platform 50 happened, support and guidance for the young women at the time she needed it, and she will be going off to university in the near future to continue her studies. What an achievement! She did it! No one else. She just needed the right support at the right time to help her do it. This is what Platform 50 was able to provide her so that she could make decisions and take actions to live the life she wanted.

In corporate business, how many people are able to say something similar to, "I need to have a day off since I'm feeling really anxious about something" without fear of being judged or penalised? Quite often, people can't afford to take time off either as they aren't given sick pay at the rate needed to pay bills or other financial commitments, if they are given sick pay at all. Others may be financially supported to take the time off that they need; however, they may feel pressured to keep going to make sure all of their work is done—or feel that they have to rectify a mistake they have made, which ends up putting them under more pressure. All of these things can affect the mental health of an individual or an organisation. What would help here is if people were supported to achieve the things they needed to do so that both personal and professional worlds could feel stable and secure. For example, I've recently become aware of a situation within an organisation where an employee was attacked by a patient when doing an assessment. She was alone in the building at the time and the patient had made threats towards her and had physically tried to harm her. Fortunately, she was able to reach her phone and lock herself in another room whilst she alerted the police about the situation she was in. The patient continued to damage the environment and shout threats to the employee who stayed in hiding. The police arrived and was able to arrest the man and reassure the employee, yet it left her understandably very shaken. This situation had affected the employee so much that she felt traumatised and scared to return to work. What she needed was time off to process what had happened and procedures to be reviewed by the organisation to make sure the likelihood of this situation reoccurring was minimised. Sadly, she was faced with having to make the decision to return to work or not be paid, so she returned to work and remains anxious about what she may experience. Whilst it's impossible for me to know the full details of this situation, I do understand mental health and how an experience like this can affect it. The employee's ability to complete her role effectively will be informed by her state of mind. This is true for any employee in any job role. If you want my advice, get out of any job that is killing you and start living your true potential.

I would like to live in a society where you can just name these things without such fear or pressures being placed on you and receive the support you need. Pay attention to your strengths and look for opportunities. I'm really interested in working with businesses that want to help support the mental health of their employees and look for people's unique abilities. My companies have already started to work in this area that has so much more to do to help guide the changes we need as a society. These changes require a whole system approach. Businesses' investment to support its employees is required, both financially and in terms of agreed change to the attitude of "that's the way things are done around here" or the secret conversations occurring about others, rather than with others. Businesses will get more productivity, employee engagement and retention for certain.

Small adjustments can have a big impact. For example, I often say to the people I employ, I want you to have a lunchtime, at lunchtime. It's a priority for you. And it's not to be used for starting the working day later or finishing it earlier, or even rush off to an appointment sometime during the day; it's to take a break, eat and refresh before the afternoon. I want the team to have sharper focus and take care of themselves in life—not just in the hours they are working for me but all of the time. This helps to develop good role models for others to follow suit and it's what we promote to the people using services in the businesses.

I've shared the story of my experience of needing time off when my granddad got ill once and I needed a few days off. I was told, "If you don't come in, it's going down as an unauthorised absence." I felt betrayed by my employer that I had devoted my skills and time to. I had also supported the individual manager personally and professionally for the good of the services we were providing, which seemed to count for nothing. And most importantly, I felt sad that I couldn't be there for my family. I had been forced to choose a one-off support for my granddad or a disciplinary at work so I tried to do both and neither went well. That was a mental health service by the way....

I want to emphasise a few points here: I had often worked beyond my hours and generally did a good job, and they knew it. I think my manager had lost sight for a moment, most probably preoccupied with all of the tasks she needed to get done. I recall a conversation with her much later, in fact when I was leaving the organisation, she said, "I don't think you've had the proper opportunity here to shine your light." This could have been her way of apologising. I'm not sure and I never asked what she meant. I kept regular contact with her after I left the organisation and we occasionally catch up with one another. I didn't take what happened personally. I just promised myself I would never be put in that situation again or respond in the compliant way that I did at the time. I'm really good at forgiveness because I'm not going to hold onto something that is going to make me feel bad or leave me feeling resentful towards someone for what they have said or how they have behaved. This is a good approach for any situation. It takes practice to learn true forgiveness. When I asked for organisational assistance, the HR department nor the organisation as a whole did anything to try and help resolve the dilemma. I can't be sure why it happened; after all, it wasn't an unreasonable request. I gave up trying to figure it out a long time ago. Maybe they labelled me as a "troublemaker" when I started to ask questions (also known as a "change maker"). What couldn't be denied was my record of performance and attendance. My commitment to the organisation. And the lack of regard for my request for help, which resulted in me rushing away from my granddad, crying at my desk and not doing what I needed to do personally or professionally.

This was the epiphany that took me on the last part of my journey to do more of what I loved and less of what I didn't, my journey to becoming totally and wholly me. I'm truly thankful for the experience. #beme

## Safeguarding and Promoting Welfare

I've been keeping up with the news about Scotland's mental health nurse shortage. Wait times for youth to get help have soared. Youths who need intervention are not getting it.

The pressures are the same in England. The NHS was set up to be free at the point of delivery and provides exceptional care and treatment to people, whether you have money or not, which differs to many other countries, although we are starting to see more and more exclusions to what is deemed entitlement in the UK (NHS, 2019). Universal healthcare is provided by many countries, some of which I've listed here; Australia; Canada; Denmark; France; Germany; Iceland; Ireland; Netherlands; New Zealand; Norway; Singapore; Sweden; Switzerland. An exception to this is the United States. Many of these countries operate a tiered healthcare provision and require financial contribution of those accessing it. In England we have a standard "referral to treatment" (RTT) time, which is an 18-week target from referral to first treatment; everyone has to be seen within that time, or there are financial penalties, reputational damage and pressures from commissioning bodies. These pressures mean that people don't always get what they need. This has encouraged organisations to consider carefully how they interpret and display their data. It has also meant that the "treatment" that people access may not always be what they need as various Directors refer to the *Commissioning Rulebook* (2016) to justify what is provided. What I want to convey here is that people can be creative with data such as RTT reporting to make it look good because it's just figures at the end of the day. It doesn't serve people well. I think until we look at how we measure outcomes and reporting for services provided by organisations, this will be a challenge to change for the better and will continue to be a disservice to the public whilst it isn't considered. It could be argued in society that we are knowingly failing to offer the help and guidance that people need at the time they need it. We only have to look at serious case reviews and incidents over the last sixty years to see these common issues highlighted.

Looking at the detail of what level of care was administered to people is significant monitoring, along with asking questions such as, "Did it directly help the person in need?" As I've said, organisations get put under pressure to achieve targets against standards. Responding by giving someone a leaflet isn't treatment in my opinion, nor is moving people from one waiting list to another, and I know some markers are being recorded and reported in this way by some services. Lots of people can confirm this although remain silent for fear of the consequences of reporting the facts—people who have been referred into services don't feel they've had treatment because they "received a leaflet" and problems deteriorate whilst they wait to long for the help they need. This approach does not safeguard people within populations in relation to health or care. Nor does it promote a good message to those employed to carry out this work and something needs to be done to change this persistent culture, which will then enable communities to get the help they need when they need it, for more than just the few. It's time to speak honestly so that the true extent of the issues can be addressed. This will remain a challenge whilst people fear losing their jobs, finance and contracts and being blamed.

Pressures can show up as staff absence, too. It's important to remember that not all physical health problems stem from something that is wrong with the body and sometimes no amount of tests can identify the cause of the problem. Sometimes a mental health problem is causing the physical illness although the symptoms may appear like physical concerns only and much easier to talk about in this way. For example, can you say, "I need two weeks off of work because I feel so overwhelmed?" That's a hard thing to say to yourself, let alone the company that employs you. I've also heard stories from people about when they had courageously stated to someone in charge that they were taking some time off of work because of their mental health needs, resulting in the person in charge keeping the information a secret, telling the workplace that the time off was due to a cold, because they don't want the person off of work to be judged for stating what they feel. This is obviously coming from a place of concern; however, it does indicate that there is some work to do to help reduce stigma within the workplace, which is something my companies assist with frequently.

I recently learned that someone who called in sick to an organisation, claiming it was due to a cold, was actually experiencing high anxiety and couldn't function on a day-to-day basis so she took some time off. Later, she was asked about the cold by her colleagues and then had to keep the lie going. She didn't want to fabricate a story, she had created it because she didn't want to discuss how things had overwhelmed her to the point that she knew she couldn't go to work and perform. Sometimes people may not speak the truth because they don't know how to do it without fear of being judged. Sometimes, they find it hard to be confident enough to say it out loud so prefer to talk about it in a physical sense. This is something we can all help to change by speaking our own truths and not fear discrimination when we do. Easier said than done I know. It does help having an independent person available within organisations and is a role I have taken on numerous occasions, as have others employed by my companies.

There are ways that organisations can help to promote mental health in the workplace and communities we live in. What do you think about mental health fitness as a culture to adopt? For example, could corporations give employees twenty minutes in a day for a walk or time outside within the working day? Could employees work out in the morning and start work later in the day, recognising the balance and health aspects this could bring?

Mental health is on a continuum. It's on a sliding scale that runs from good mental health to mental illness, which can be affected by experiences. For example, I could be due to take an exam or have a workplace deadline one morning and that could affect my mental health before, during and after it. I could have a birthday party planned and that could affect my mental health leading up to it, during it and once it's over. Mental health could vary at different parts of the day, just as physical health could. You have to work at maintaining good mental health with things like sleeping regularly, eating healthy most of the time, and not emailing in the middle of the night through fear or pressure about finishing work.

It's simple really. If you can be mentally healthy, you can enjoy life and you can function. You can develop resilience, bounce back from things that don't go so well. Life is full of ups and downs, situations and experiences—some good and some not so. Good mental health will help you know that it's not because you're worthless or to blame. Failure is not finality...in anything really. It's part of life and can be learned from and help develop you as a person or organisation. What is important is how people and organisations apply the learning in any situation arising. Blaming one person for something that a whole system needs to address is not beneficial, nor is blaming yourself. As human beings, we all cross into that negative self-talk like a live wire, which chips away at us, chips away at our self-love. It's something that L.O.V.E Leadership can assist to change although it's not always an easy road to travel. That's why the support of coaches and mentors is invaluable. It really is worth investing in yourself to help you pay attention to your strengths.

The book *Mastering Your Inner Critic...and 7 Other High Hurdles to Advancement*, by leadership development consultant, Susan MacKenty Brady, considers negative self-talk and says, "You may ignore it for a little while, but at your most vulnerable times (for instance, when you're feeling stressed, insecure, unhappy, exhausted or unclear), an inner voice expresses judgment, frustration, or at its most extreme, harshness and contempt. This inner voice can be instructive, and clue us into some feelings or thoughts that might be helpful as we navigate life and relationships."

I have experience of that voice and have helped others with similar experiences. It can be quite harsh and may feel like it's taking over. Brady recommends trying to get to a "compassionate centre." Simply pausing to tell yourself that you are good enough in that moment and breathe deeply in that knowledge. Let that message drown out the inner critic. Shrink the obstacles that get in the way of your success. After all, your best capabilities got you here.

As part of my journey I knew I had to improve my level of self-confidence in order to know that I am good enough, which has included knowing that I am good at the work that I do, too. Within organisations people seek to apportion blame, which is an unhealthy way to function. I've heard phrases used such as "I'll take the hit for this failing situation, I'm nearly retired so I can go now," "she took her eye off the ball" or "they want blood for this, we better give them something (or someone)." It's a destructive way of functioning and requires support to change before there are any more casualties.

I've seen people reduced to tears after being stripped of their senior position because things have *gone wrong* at work. I've never been passive in these circumstances and have challenged the culture and the overall decision makers about these occurrences because things can never be one person's fault. The action of others says a great deal about their own development needs. I've know that I'm good at my job roles because I have an open heart and I care about all people; it's just how I see things. I'm passionate, honest and I feel happy to be alive, living this life, helping others. It really is amazing! This doesn't mean I don't have experiences that hurt or upset me. Everyone has bad days that are part of life's twists and turns! What's important here is how you use those experiences and learn things to make changes and shape the future, which you may need help to do.

Travelling a journey of L.O.V.E Leadership may feel daunting or like something you want to avoid doing. You may not see how it could be relevant to your business. Regardless, I would say do it anyway. Be prepared to feel vulnerable and exposed in order for a greater good. Consider that every time I reveal something personal about myself, I have no idea what the response will be, whether it's from one person, a board room, a conference podium. Sometimes it's about sharing that uncomfortable internal dialogue with someone. It's not half as bad when you share it. Don't give up. Even when it feels challenging, remember that you are an equal to anyone else. It takes practice and I believe you can achieve anything that you put your mind to. Then encourage people to step outside their comfort zone and do something different to make a change for themselves. This is what helps organisations, too.

## Group Strength, Not Groupthink

I have an interest in whole systems and have studied and experienced these intensively—in companies and in families. There are similarities in what you may do in an organisational system and within a family unit, though it does not always match fully. As a society, we talk a lot about things going wrong, focusing on negativity and drama. This is portrayed via the media and online in many different ways. Life is a soap opera, and that is why soap operas get so many viewings; we know that they are dramatized, but basically a great deal of it is still true to life. So let's consider, how does breaking news impress upon our psyches? Let's start by discussing business. I want to focus on what's going right and build things upon that, and this doesn't mean that we avoid problems or concerns. It does mean there is a need for support and challenge conversations within organisations and people need some assistance to have these conversations. What could go right if we just apply this approach to ourselves individually? How can you change yourself to be an influencer within business?

Many people may become stuck and unhelpful in their own search for happiness. For example, if you think you have the worst job and the system you work in is ineffective, do something about it. Don't just complain about it at every opportunity. Likewise, if you are someone who overhears these complaints, address them at the time. This can help avoid unhealthy cliques from forming or blame, criticism or scapegoating occurring, which can develop as part of team formation and group dynamics. Be aware that speaking up isn't always a popular choice as people may not want to feel confronted or corrected and because of this, some people may fear speaking out and being a lone voice. However, we do know that complaining and gossiping about others isn't conducive to a good working environment so it is beneficial for individuals and teams to have opportunities to speak openly. This is even more important within smaller teams, although crucial for every team. For example, I have worked within a small charity where the leadership group met four times a year, when they could be bothered to turn up. At that meeting there had already been several conversations to "lobby" for support on a view or decision that someone in the group wanted to make, after talking about each other behind closed doors, rather than having open discussions at the meetings. Relationships within that group were poor and mistrusting. Honest conversations were not encouraged, and if you attempted this, you became a perceived threat. This climate had continued for over 10 years. Everyone had an opinion about everyone else and made judgements about perceived failings. These conversations happened about each other, not with each other, justified behaviours, and everyone took a role in the spotlight at one time or another. The very thing that was needed was the thing that would not be tolerated. Key individuals believed they had all the answers and did not work together for the good of the organisation. This filtered down into the team where people felt able to gossip about others or behave badly towards colleagues. It became an unkind place to work where people justified their behaviours. These behaviours were so entrenched, they became invisible to the group.

I have experienced something similar in other organisations, too. I remember a team manager who used to speak about people in a derogatory way. She had names for people which she used when talking with other members of the senior leadership team, who laughed and joined in. This had gone unaddressed for many years until I was employed to help the team improve. I started to address some of the behaviours, which resulted in a revengeful attack on me by her. The people she had been unpleasant about had supported her, not realising that her manipulation had placed her as the victim in the situation and added to "group think." I was never able to have this open conversation with the whole group because I moved on in my role whilst she took a period of time off of work. I do believe addressing this unwanted behaviour was the key to many of the issues that the team there faced and continue to face. Of course, what people think of others is their business. However, this had become an unhealthy dynamic, which put others in a group against an individual. Gossip can *crumble* whole organisations. Effective groups of people or teams can *build* organisations.

If every individual was working in a key set of principles in line with L.O.V.E Leadership, recognising that people would be at different stages of their journey, can you imagine the positive impact this would have? Over the years I have met many wonderful people who have a great amount of empathy and love to give. It's amazing to see this in action. If someone has a voice and I have a voice, we can have a powerful conversation. If we're actively listening more than waiting to talk, fantastic. If we're acting with integrity and empowering others rather than disempowering them, what's not to love? We must be prepared to *own* the part we play in our lives and in organisations. This can be promoted at an early age so that people don't have to learn L.O.V.E Leadership, just live it.

Early experiences develop who we become. People continue to compare themselves to others as they have always done. I feel sad to see some fabulous people put themselves down or doubt themselves. These are the people who I like to show how amazing they are and empower them to believe that, too. Our experiences and our parents' experiences and their parents' experiences, and so on, shape us. Family context and culture is significant in this *systemic* view. When I'm working with businesses and helping them to improve, I'm thinking systemically. It's important to consider the whole system because you have to work with it all; see the big picture. If people learned much more confidence and belief in themselves to like who they are, even if that is not the same as others, from a much an early age, they would be able to identify when they're not being treated with care and respect so they could stop it. And vice versa. Think about it. What happens when someone treats you poorly or with disrespect? What do you do? Can you freely approach them to discuss it or do you internalise the experience and start to feel bad about yourself? Or do you gossip?

"Intergenerational changes" are something needed to tackle repeating patterns of behaviours within individuals and family units. I really want to help change that because I can see the relevance of this in every aspect of life. It's surprising how far back it goes, and looking at the bigger picture, if one part isn't working effectively, then it's all broken. This is what helped me to name one of the companies I founded. Arterne advocates "enriching the next generation." Meaning, it's "our turn." Our own turn to make a difference. As a company we can also help to make a difference in the lives of people who are growing up right now by getting alongside them much earlier and offering something alternative for them to think about. For example, if I can bring up my daughter to be happy and healthy, if she goes on to have children, she will know how to bring them up to have aspirations and to strive for their happiness. This cannot be accomplished in isolation. Conversation helps shape the success of this.

I've worked with groups of families in which each family unit has one adult member dying. This understandably impacts upon the family group dynamic. I recall they were engrossed in an activity together, making crafts and I remember thinking, *I don't know if I will see all of these people next week.* They were there with their children and we were supporting them make everlasting memories so they have them to recall when the special person has died. When this happens isn't predictable, so we could never be sure what would happen for the family between group sessions each week. All we knew was their family unit will likely be very different without that person being there, and talking about it helped.

Expressing feelings, creating memories and learning to cope is how I helped to categorised the areas needing to be focused on. This enables the family to be able to deal with their grief and loss in healthy ways. I refer to this as the *cycle of acceptance* and it is important for individuals and family systems to understand so they can make sense of some of their thoughts and feelings. I don't think you can ever truly prepare for death or terminal illness and what that brings. You can impact positively on levels of resilience.

## Business Strategy and Mental Health

I've had several role models or influencers throughout my life. One of these people was a professor and trained clinical psychologist who went onto become a specialist in leadership practices, teamwork and systems, completing his Ph.D. on Community Mental Health

Teams. I was fortunate enough to be coached by him and attend many of his trainings over a number of years. I really admired him and I was deeply saddened to learn of his death almost four years ago whilst he was completing a charity bike ride. This man had a high level of integrity and has touched the lives of many in a very positive way. I would say "I got my wings" while participating in a program called "Leadership for All of You." It was over a weekend in Bristol, which is where he lived. The program was established between him and a colleague. I had to attend a weekend of intensive days combining leadership and shadow work for a small group of people. This took place just right before I set my business up as a registered company. It was a weekend that ran high with emotions. I had already done a lot of transformative work before I attended the course, whereas others were at a different stage of their journey and shared a lot about themselves. The weekend included role-play, *the five elements* of the world, practical activities and deep discussion. Part of the weekend process included writing a letter to yourself in the future tense (one year's time), talking about your achievements at that point. It's important to consider the best year of your life and aim for that. Then you can start living on purpose.

The course leaders kept the letter in a sealed envelope after the course and they posted it out to you in one year's time. That's when I made the decision to start my own company. The whole experience was amazing and it consolidated my previous personal and professional development, leading me further into my journey.

During the course, I had thought about how I had been bullied in my previous job for thinking and speaking differently. And for being a lone voice in doing the right thing. This experience has also highlighted my social class and difference. It's all had a significant impact on me over the years. I have working-class roots, which I'm proud of, but has been a subject of negative judgements. For example, my experiences in the boardroom and in senior positions within some organisations, this approach can be considered "outspoken" and isn't always encouraged. I'm not always what people may expect to find and have been advised on many occasions that I need to learn to "play the game" or join the "in" group.

I recall one experience when a consultant said to me, "Cindy, are you surprised where you ended up?"—which was code for, "How on earth did you get this job?" At the time, I was too shocked to say anything other than, "No. Are you?" Needless to say, there were a key group of people within the team that had worked in a fixed way for a long period of time.

I think it's important to be aware that there is a huge amount of *group think*. There are suggestions that tribal and pack mentality has become more pronounced as we spend more time online. Empathy is the ability to step into the shoes of someone else and see things from their point of view. It also helps to understand difference. This is not something that all individuals, teams or organisations are attuned too. I've always strived to do is do the right thing for the people using the services, placing them at the centre of the experience, so things can be shaped to have a positive impact. This hasn't always been welcomed by some employees within organisations. This is usually a reaction to the notion of change, which does have to be managed sensitively. I've never been afraid of change or saying the unpopular thing for the good of people using services. It's not always been welcomed with open arms, which is something I have come to terms with in favour of doing the right thing.

For companies and "systems," I have spent a lot of time emphasising safeguarding and promoting welfare. The factors range from emotional and behavioural development and social presentation, to family history and functioning, to emotional warmth and guidance and boundaries—this is indeed, the core of life as we know it. I fundamentally believe that systems thinking can more closely ensure that individuals have each of the needs met. The more people whose needs are met across this spectrum, the greater the world's mental health can be maintained.

## WELLNESS WARRIOR

**Diana Guy, Founder, Relax International**

A prime systems thinker is Diana Guy, who, as of this writing, is in her forty-sixth year teaching yoga and meditation in the United States.

Her programs of "chaos to calm" have helped various populations, including victims of domestic violence, cancer patients, pre-schoolers, at-risk youth, people in recovery from problematic substance use, athletes, and high-performing executives. She is a firm believer in mental healthiness through yoga and meditation, starting with your first breath of the day. Here, she answers a few questions about her profession's surprising outcomes.

**Q: Why did you first seek yoga and meditation as a student and then decide to teach?**

**A:** Since 1973, my initial entry into yoga was a night out and Lilias Folan, the famous yoga teacher on TV at that time, and it was a relaxation class. Relaxation was so profound for me. Out of 65 people, I was sure I was the only one having chaotic half-sentences in my head and I was so anxious, which I had not noticed before. My body was so stiff and sore. Realising all this was so sad to my psyche and body at the young age of 23. Yoga was popular in the early 1970s and her TV show (aired 29 years) was one reason it was gaining popularity. So instead of running from that anxiety, I looked at it and decided to go back each week for a 10-week session. I wrote in my journal about it and was taken in by her. She became an amazing mentor during that time for me. Very nurturing and off to New York I went to the yoga seminary to meet with her and her teachers from India and studied all aspects of yoga and meditation. Then I began traveling with her and teaching, subbing for her and offering my own classes and workshops. In 1975, other teachers and I began the Cincinnati Yoga Association, which is still one of the largest in the world, which I am so proud of. We helped mentor other associations from overseas and around the States to help each other and have a sense of community and social network.

My first time teaching was actually in our neighbourhood. My kids and their friends would get off the bus and come to my house and I would teach yoga in the afternoon. It calmed them and soothed them from the day. That was my initial teaching—elementary school. It was amazing to see their chaotic energy after school slow down from the stretching and the stillness. They would shift from their temper tantrum and eating disorders, which we didn't really note at that time. Grades 1 to 7. Then I started teaching in other elementary schools and high schools in religion and health classes. Then colleges like Mt. Saint Joseph. A friend published a book, *Yoga for Kids*, and had a PBS series, along with Lilias's program. Now I teach my grandkids all of this. I was immersed in that ancient practice, but within me was all this quivering to share it in a new way.

In the early 80s, I developed a family health program where I would teach family units. The whole family was involved and it was quite remarkable.

From that, the drug and alcohol rehab. A friend had trouble with alcoholism so I found out about this residential facility and created a program of yoga and meditation. Then the cancer wellness program later on in the 90s. I worked with cancer patients and their families and still do today, over 20 years now.

**Q: How might your practice relate to L.O.V.E Leadership?**

**A:** Here is the thread in all of this regarding depression and the suicide rates. Those components are within. The cancer group, who have been diagnosed, the families who are caretakers to people affected by substances, to people who are abused, and prenatal—the anxiety, fears, drama or any trauma—accident or self-imposed, all of that is woven into any of these groups. What the yoga and meditation is able to do is gently start to release where that is held in the body, start to release the held breath. As I always say, we hold our breath more than we breathe, and we don't realise that! You have to begin releasing the breath. In a class, it's more subtle. In a private session, the results are more dramatic because you can really dive into the individual experience. Hormonal imbalance is also a symptom that is helped.

Coinciding with Emily Conrad's work, Continuum Movement, her expertise is noting that we're so lacking a sense of intimacy, even within ourselves and love for ourselves. That was in the 1980s that I studied this. Here we are in 2018, and I was just mentioning this in my class for Procter & Gamble employees, with the Internet and phones, how we are even more disconnected today than we were in the 80s, unable to communicate (or we do with short half-sentences or emojis). That staccato rhythm in how we text shifts our brain. We become filled with tension and anxiety and we don't realise it. It's our norm! Thus, the suicide rates. We get in a chaotic mess and we don't know how to deal with it, so that is our way out. Look at our news cycle. It keeps us in a state of flux of chaos. I keep thinking it can't get any worse and then I see a piece on Trump last night making fun of sexual abuse against women? I was flabbergasted this morning. I held my breath, realising that and how driving to work to teach people how to be calm and present, I was tense in my body. I put on new age music before I got there and arrived early, so I could just pause and be with everyone as they came in.

**Q: Talking about chaos, I want to give you two disturbing scenarios:**

**1. According to WHO, approximately 1 million people commit suicide every year worldwide. In the U.S. suicides have escalated year after year for the last 15 years.**
**2. "Lockdown, lockdown, lock the door. Shut the lights off, say no more." In the state of Massachusetts in the US, a class of five-year-olds are learning this rhyme, set to the lullaby "Twinkle, Twinkle, Little Star," so they know what to do during a school shooting.**

**How do we reverse all this and come into our calm?**

**A:** We're missing that connection with ourselves, first and foremost. It's like that experience of me the very first night in the relaxation class—I saw and felt my body so uptight and my short, little half sentences, which weren't connected at all, rambling in my mind. I never noticed that. That is our field we walk and move and live in and we don't realise it until you're in that relaxation and you start to feel calm. Then you have a relationship with being calm and in balance and peaceful and lighter and less anxious and less depressed and less anger. Less held tight jaws and hips and pelvic areas, less heart attacks. It goes on and on. Until you start to release those held breaths. Yoga is the most balanced tool of all holistic modalities out there. That and continuum movement. I have both under my experiential belt here for healing. I don't know what I would do without it! I can't imagine having survived without my yoga. The simple moves in yoga effect the endocrine glands. Your endocrine system affects your whole body chemically and biologically. That balancing effect to the mind and heart that no other modality has. That is what is so remarkable about yoga when it is taught properly and with alignment and the depths of understanding it. Today, there are many watered down versions and variations, so to get someone with that depth of experience and knowledge is so important to facilitate these changes.

**Q: How do you approach someone with mental illness with your techniques?**

**A:** Obviously they have to request help. First of all, they have to acknowledge it, or as you say, 'Own'. If they come to me for a private session or share that in the class, I recommend a private session. If we're in a workshop on depression and anxiety, the simple way to begin is for them to notice that they're holding their breath, how their posture is reflective, how they are rounding their shoulders, how their necks are turned downward, eyes usually down. The breath is so shallow if it's at all. Their concave chest. There is a whole posture reflective of different degrees of depression. Just by increasing the breath a few moments, you begin to unfold that body. I get goose bumps every time I see this. It's amazing to me—how simple this is, how simple we are and how profound that simple work is. Breath is the key.

**Q: What does hope mean to you?**

**A:** It's connected with the breath in that when I deepen my inhalation, when I take that deep breath in, that is me inviting in something new. That gives me hope. Each inhalation is the new coming in. Each exhalation I'm focused on my ability to let go, let go of stuff I don't want, let go of my frozen shoulder, let go of a tense conversation last evening, a disappointment last evening, all of this stuff to that circle and cycle of breath, breathing in something new. If I focus my intention with that, the depression will fade away immediately. It sounds so simple, but it really, truly is that simple. It requires practice and first acknowledging. Even with people who are dying, I was just with my sister before she died. I sat with her and breathed with her. In that life-giving process of breath, that is our umbilical cord to all of life itself. My hope is all the people on this planet just realising how simple this is, to take deeper breaths and your ability to let go—what a profound experience. There would no longer be any discord or harm. Nonviolence would exist. That whole potential is there within a breath. That still fascinates me! It is a very organic realisation of hope and harmony. It is an affirmation for world peace, or peace within yourself or your community or your family, friends, those who you have had discord with. It is phenomenal for me to see this. It is beautiful to see people change their state of affairs from the chaos to the calm.

## L.O.V.E Leadership in Action

How are you feeling? Well, it's about to get more exciting for all of us, as L.O.V.E makes way and makes waves.

I'm often asked about the process of L.O.V.E Leadership. "Cindy, we can tell people to love yourself, strive for better, but what does this look like?"

L.O.V.E Leadership is a simple acronym: *listen; own; voice; empower.* It is about being able to have an honest conversation with yourself and think about how you conduct yourself as a leader. A leader of you! We all have internal dialogue that we listen to. It is about hearing it and knowing what to do with it—when to use it and when not to. If it's critical or derogatory to you it will be unhelpful to go on listening to that, just as listening to someone who speaks to you in a disrespectful way. However, we have to act with caution here as how much are we projecting into a conversation or experience which results in us shaping things negatively for ourselves. Remember your roots. Voice is as significant in communications as listening. For example, when you sit in a meeting and you say something, perhaps there is an internal dialogue that voice says, *You just made an idiot of yourself!*

L.O.V.E Leadership is also about challenging that and negative self-talk. Knowing who you are being in any given moment helps with this and you need to be prepared to hear the voice of another person. Empowerment can be achieved through *engaging, educating* to *evolve.* Empowering someone else is also about the intention behind the action you take or words you say. Integrity is important here and is defined well for me by *doing the same thing when no one is looking.*

Consider:,How have you become you? Who are you being in any moment? Are you being your mum, dad, gran, sibling, someone else? Have you remained focused on looking for a negative experience? How are you influencing a situation that you are unhappy with?

I understand this is a lot to think about and I don't want you to blame yourself. I want you to be honest and accepting. Your history shows you who you are. It takes practice to change that and do something different.

Let's look at this in more detail!

# Chapter 7

## *Listen*

I RECALL TAKING A JOURNEY ON a train to London where I sat next to someone who told me about her brother having mental health issues. She told me that he had also become suicidal at one point, which she found hard to understand. I didn't know the woman I sat next to. We had met partway through my journey. It was a two-hour train ride and in that short period of time, I had learned a lot about her life story. This is not a single experience to me. I often find myself in conversation with people I don't know who confide in me and then they sometimes feel disbelief that they've shared this personal information.

I'm a great believer in a "problem shared is a problem halved.".If you make yourself available and open to listening, people will tell you things about their lives, what's troubling them or others. You can help people by being present and listening. It's such a powerful experience that you may have been fortunate enough to experience for yourself or have provided for others.

There are other people that I meet who do not place value on conversation. They can be avoidant in engaging in conversation about anything outwardly. However, this does not stop the internal dialogue that occurs and is something that everyone experiences, which can be damaging if it is a critical or negative voice. A lot of my work is about conversations and for some, these conversations have healing properties. This can be a hard concept to promote as it is conversational and experiential rather than something you can grasp hold of or take as a medicine that will make people feel better. When you purchase something practical, you know what you will get out of it, whereas if you are paying for a conversation there is still an unknown about its impact so you may not want to make the investment. Encouraging people to invest in themselves is important yet remains a challenge for people to agree to take action. I mean this in terms of financial support as well as an investment of time for themselves.

In my time spent treating people through auricular acupuncture, I was able to offer a space for conversation at the same time of them receiving their treatment, although many people had booked appointments with me to get help with their physical ailments. These conversations developed naturally in response to treating people with physical symptoms, with no apparent physical cause, who, after finding a way to have open dialogue with me, started to notice a reduction in their symptoms. For example, a woman in her sixties came for treatment of "neuralgia" after her GP was unable to provide anything to her that made a positive difference. She arrived on a windy, wet, winter's day, wearing a woolly hat and told me in depth about her pains and failed treatments. She said the hat "helped" her, so I became curious about this. We began treatment and I spent time listening to her story. This is where I learned about her lifelong struggles with anxiety, which had prevented her from going out shopping on some occasions. She had never told anyone about this before talking with me, which surprised her a little. Much to her surprise, her pains lessened and she felt able to cope with her anxiety more and became less house-bound. The combined process of treatment and conversation had significantly altered her life for the better.

Listening or learning not to listen to the physical self is equally important for health. Some people may prefer a quiet room, breathing practice and mindfulness. This also requires being in tune with you in the moment and takes practice. If you're trying to lose weight, running, going to the gym and eating properly, will you stop and contemplate which item is helping you the most? It really doesn't matter. It's the impact of the combination.

I'm often asked what makes a good mental health nurse. I always say the ability to really listen and to step into the shoes of another person is equally important and is something I am good at doing. I think needing these skills are true for many professions. I've always compared being a nurse to my earlier jobs working in bars. I have friends who work in bars and we agree that the skills are very transferable. This is because people from all walks of life visit bars and have various conversations! The model of L.O.V.E Leadership promotes listening to someone or being listened to as a powerful thing. This differs to only hearing the words. It's about making a connection. For example, if my daughter comes home tonight and I'm rushing out of the door, while texting on my phone, then I'm not listening. This experience feels different when I look her in the eye, to take time and to feel what she is saying; that is a more powerful experience for her and for me. It really makes a difference. I use it every day. Try it!

A student I've been working with who previously had a negative experience on placement said to me today, "I've had the best day, thank you!" It was lovely to hear that feedback. It felt genuine and authentic.

It's sometimes easy for professionals to forget what's important or to slip into bad habits, which means they miss what's important in their work. In my previous work, leading a children and young people's charity working to support death and dying, I was having a conversation with a member of the team who wanted to "close a case" using the rationale, "I have a dad who won't listen to me. I've tried everything. I don't think I can work with him anymore." I responded and asked her, "What does the dad want to achieve?" She hesitated, looked at me and said, "I haven't asked. I don't know. I suggest everything and he doesn't do it!"

Again, I responded to encourage her to reflect and said, "Why don't you try involving him in the conversation about what he wants to achieve?"

What became clear during this conversation was the team member, who was inexperienced in this area of work, had tried to take the position of expert and stopped listening to what the family wanted.

This is sometimes what professionals can do. In this instance, it was what was creating the communication issues and the breakdown in relationship; it was getting in the way of supporting the family with what they needed and once identified enabled the situation to take a different direction. I have always found it beneficial to listen actively first to determine where it is someone wants to be helped or supported. I may respectfully challenge things if what they are suggesting may cause them more harm. The approach taken has to be person centred and what a professional may choose for someone may not be the desired goal for the individual or family unit (there's a whole other conversation here about capacity and how this is considered or assessed). Determining goals can be helped by speaking out loud with others who are trusted, too.

For example, I recall speaking with a teenage girl. Her mother had recently died, which understandably made her feel very sad. She was accompanied to the meeting with me, by two social workers and her brother. She was getting into trouble with school for not attending. Her brother was so helpful in the conversation as when asked, "What do you think? What would you like to see happen for your sister?" he responded, "I would like to see her smile." They didn't speak this way together when they were alone. A facilitated conversation drew these words and wishes out. For her to hear that was powerful.

Friends and family members can help. A smile can open up another conversation. A sense of humour is a resilience factor and can also be used to relax a challenging conversation or even get one started.

Within companies speaking about people negatively, making judgements or gossiping can impact on team functioning significantly and can even cause structures to crumble. This behaviour can be magnified within smaller teams and businesses than in larger because of its impact. Group process attempts to explain how individuals behave within group situations. There are specific roles identified and played out within groups that are often unconscious. However, these behaviours say much more about the people behaving in these ways. It's true that human beings talk about each other, but the intention behind this is always worth considering. Being curious about something someone says about another person's behaviours or conversations is a healthy approach. The best way to tackle this is to stop the conversation taking place in front of you or to simply not listen to it and to make up your own mind about the situation or person. Lots of people find it hard to do this and it does takes practice.

I avoid conversations with people that I would not be prepared to have in front of people. Build on strengths. Talk about the good in people. And be prepared to challenge and be open about what's needing to be different, with good intentions. Unfortunately, we cannot always take things at face value; this can be a good starting position. Some people may not appreciate the direct approach and they will require some support to understand it. This is true within business and in families. Sometimes this is the most beneficial approach to take.

## L.O.V.E LEADERSHIP IN ACTION

### Gina and David Smallridge, Care Home Owners

Following an inspection by the regulators for health and social care, CQC, the care home had been considered to be seriously failing in all Key Lines of Enquiry (KLOEs) in August 2017. This resulted in the care home being placed into special measures and closed to admissions.

Gina said, "This came as a great shock to me as the Registered Provider and to my husband as the Nominated Individual. For over 18 years, we had passed all regulatory inspections and held an excellent reputation in the city.

"CQC inspectors had received concerns from the Adult Safeguarding teams also, which meant the care home had to address concerns on an emergency basis.

"The care home was closed to admissions, which resulted in a huge financial worry for us, too. Income fell because we weren't able to fill vacant beds as they arose. Assessments were being done to try and find residents new homes. Making improvements put an even bigger financial strain on us and we worked hard to keep staff employed and to avoid redundancies.

“A member of the safeguarding team gave me Cindy’s number. She was known by the safeguarding team as she had successfully supported other care homes in a similar situation to us.

“On meeting Cindy for the first time it was evident she was very experienced and was able to work with us to put an action plan together to achieve the set standards. This action plan had to be presented to the Health Care Commissioners, Social Services and CQC. Cindy fully supported us through this process, which included monthly updates to the action plan and the presentations. Cindy was also able to put in two Registered Nurses to work alongside the care home staff teams, supporting them improving documentation and communication. This also gave emotional support to staff who were very stressed with the situation the care home was in, the possibility the home could close and the worry that they could lose their jobs.

“With Cindy’s continuity of guidance and support, including the two nurses, a calm and professional attitude was taken by everyone in putting the action plan in place. Six months following the initial CQC inspection, another inspection took place. The care home was taken out of special measures and business was able to continue with controlled admissions. Cindy’s experience of mental health, supported by her L.O.V.E Leadership model of listening and empowerment of staff, in particular, was evident in her approach in supporting the care home and us as Manager and Provider. She understood the stress and anxiety the situation was causing us. A calm and positive attitude was encouraging, always available to listen and discuss concerns, working together towards positive outcomes, soon became evident the action plan was achievable.

“Mental health issues should be made more public. Education regarding mental health should be recognised as equally as physical health and not seen as a taboo subject. For the population of older people our business cares for, we would like to see less stereotyping of older people. The value of their skills and experience should be acknowledged and they should be seen as an asset to society. Older people should be less worried about growing old with support services in place to prevent social isolation."

## Reflection From the Heart

Working with Gina and David was an absolute pleasure. The application of the L.O.V.E Leadership model helped them to achieve the standards set by the regulators. It wasn't always an easy road and there were many challenging conversations in order to make the changes required. What shone through was their care and commitment to getting it right. The experience of being inspected resulting in an inadequate rating was unexpected and there were many things to consider. Collectively, we had to listen to what was being said by the regulators, even if we didn't agree with everything being said in the reports. That feedback was what formed the basis of the action plan that was implemented and more significantly monitored for effectiveness. I love Gina and David's approach to business, which was family orientated. I believe that L.O.V.E Leadership empowered them to do what they had always been able to do, which was lead good quality services.

I recently received a message from Gina to thank me for the help and guidance we offered to them, letting me know that the care home had just been given an "outstanding" rating for care and "four goods" following their latest inspection. Hearing this news gave me an overwhelming sense of pride to be part of their journey. Gina and David had experienced something overwhelming in emotion. The situation almost cost them their business. They never gave up. They used what was happening at the time to motivate themselves to keep going and continue to provide good quality care for people.

# Chapter 8

## *Own*

EVERYONE IS SHAPED BY WHAT they do with the experiences they have. This is different to being shaped by your experiences. Does it make sense to you? How the experiences you have impact on your life is about how you interpret it and what you do with it. Is that clearer to you now? Let's look at this in more detail.

In the model of L.O.V.E Leadership, "own" refers to "ownership" of your life. It is about remembering your roots. As noted before, some people may call it baggage, but I believe it can only be baggage that will laden you down if you only let the experience influence your thoughts, feelings and behaviours, rather than what you do with that experience.

*Ownership is an empowering interpretation of what has happened to you.* It places the control of your experience with you. It is also encourages you to consider how your experiences do shape you and your behaviour and as a result, what you may interpret in a conversation or experience. Becoming aware of what you project out as a result of your family culture, relationships and experiences is important and often something that people need help to achieve. Owning your own stuff begins with an acceptance by you. Then comes being prepared to share it to help others take the same journey. I'm not talking about bearing your heart and soul to everyone you meet. Nor am I suggesting that you express every detail about your life with others. It's more about the journey of acceptance and not fearing judgement about these experiences. Own is about taking the learning from these experiences, which you will need resilience to do. It also helps to have a trusted coach or mentor.

I recall a situation I experienced whilst working at a drug and alcohol rehabilitation service where I had a role to facilitate leadership and support required improvements. A woman had been admitted for treatment at a time when other people staying at the house were planning to go away on a residential experience elsewhere. The rehab staff said they weren't aware that the woman would arrive on this particular day so hadn't done any of the planning for it. I had taken the original call to confirm the date and it was written in the office diary so it was something the rehab had overlooked or not communicated effectively, rather than being unaware of it as they claimed. It caused real confusion and created a negative experience for the woman who had arrived for treatment. She was in her late sixties. She had physical health problems, had just finished a detox and did not want to go on the camping trip unexpectedly. I was intrigued by what happened next. Rather than listen to the woman and respect her wishes, the counsellor thought they could talk her into it and "would not stop" until she agreed to go. As you can imagine, this approach did not result in a good outcome. In my opinion, there was no necessity for her to go, there were other options to explore. The only challenge was the counsellor seeing the situation as a battle of wills between the rehab and the woman. The conversation continued for some time and in my opinion the rehab lost sight of the real reason the woman was there, which was to recover from a lifelong struggle with substances.

At one point during the conversation the woman asked, "Where is the camping trip?" Instead of using this as an opportunity to inform her of the benefits of the trip and engage her, the response she got was, "Why do you want to know?"

I'm sure you can figure out how this situation ended. The woman replied, "Because I'm not a child", and so the conflict continued.

So just reflect for a moment. What do you think was happening here?

I observed that the woman wasn't heard, she wasn't enabled to have a voice, people used their voices to tell her what was going to happen and were unable to step into her shoes to see it from her point of view. She wasn't empowered. The counsellor also didn't *own* their own stuff in this situation.

My experience of the woman was that she was so lovely. I didn't see her as being difficult as the team had suggested. She didn't want to do something that hadn't been planned with her, and voiced it. It didn't mean she was trying to cause problems. Unfortunately, she didn't continue with her treatment at the rehab, she moved to another one. Before she left, she had hugged me, thanking me for my help with trying to resolve the situation. The reality was all I had done was listen to her and tried to see things from her position. This should be encouraged more in order to help people affect change. People are not going to get it exactly right in the beginning, so they seek help and treatment because they can't do it alone.

After she left, my role was to challenge the rehab team with the part they played in the woman leaving treatment with them, which was partially due to *group think*. I also needed to remind people that *difference* is there to be celebrated and everyone being the same isn't healthy or representative of the world we live in. I remember saying, "You work in a drug and alcohol rehabilitation. People arriving for treatment are adults and can make choices. Within that shades of difficulty may exist, however, if people had effective coping and communication skills, or relationship skills to live a happy and healthy life, they wouldn't be here either".

It's important to consider that something unconscious may have been happening in this situation. Regardless of the reason, it resulted in a negative experience for the woman who had arrived for treatment. The team were collaborators in this experience and in my opinion, the situation could have been avoided. Maybe the woman reminded the counsellor of someone or perhaps they were being triggered by the dynamic of the interaction between them. Sometimes people interpret another person's conversation or behaviour with a meaning, which isn't an accurate assessment of the situation. As we've already established, this will all be shaped by how we use our previous experiences.

What's interesting is that people may have even worked through something which they then notice affecting them in later life. A conscious awareness of these things and an ability of being able to reflect on your own thoughts and behaviours helps you to notice what you project out.

Many professionals working with people who need help have required their own help in the past. It's important to be aware of your triggers, vulnerabilities and prejudices. This can be helpful in business. too. It's about catching something happening as it arises and then reframing it so that you can respond differently or it can impact on you differently. For example, you may have received an email that makes you feel tense and criticised. Instead of responding from an emotional place, create some space and pause for a moment. Or make a cup of tea, relax and then revisited the message before responding. It feels different. Try it! It's about having insight. You can still say what you want to say, just without the emotion of life history that sometimes still shows up for people in their personal and professional lives.

## Being In Service Feels Better!

It's a common occurrence for people who have had challenges to go on to help others with challenges, whether it's support for drug and alcohol use or anyone who has experienced mental health problems or illness. This is also true for people who have been affected by a physical illness and recovered. People will also volunteer time to good causes that may have been something which affected them in their personal lives. I'm often asked why I care so much. I have reflected on this and my belief is that I genuinely do want people to live the lives they want and be the best version of themselves that they can be. I have truly found my vocation. I often support people without charge because that is what's needed, rather than account for every last minute of my time and produce an invoice. I'll help someone anywhere in the world.

I recall many experiences of meeting people who are homeless. When I don't have any money on me to offer them, I look them in the eye and say, "I'm sorry, I don't have any money on me to give you". It feels important to do that. I don't want to be another person who drops her head, avoids eye contact and walks past without acknowledgment. I have some understanding about how it feels not to have enough money to feed yourself or pay your bills. I think it takes a lot of motivation and strength to ask someone for help, even if it's someone you don't know and may never see again. I always try and make conversation if people are open to it. I may be able to help them directly through my companies or link them up with another service that can help them.

I was walking through Hull City Centre and noticed a man propped up in the doorway. It was early in the morning and there weren't many other people around. I went over and asked him if I could buy him a hot drink and some food for breakfast, which he easily accepted. I returned with a hot drink and a selection of food that I had purchased from a nearby supermarket. He was thrilled and clearly very hungry as he ate quickly. We began to speak about things and he told me of his experiences of sleeping on the streets. Of men urinating on him whilst he slept, spitting on him, swearing and even asking for sexual favours in exchange for money. I asked him whether there was anyone he could stay with so he didn't have to sleep in the doorway another night. He told me about his father and although they didn't always get on he felt that if he could get there he could stay there to help get back on his feet. I asked him why he hadn't gone to see his dad before and it came down to the fact he didn't have £14.40 to get the bus to where his dad lived.

Are you thinking about his story like I did? I wanted to help. I didn't give him the money because I didn't have any cash on me. Instead, I agreed to meet him at the nearby bus station at a set time and said he if really wanted to go to his dad's house to get him off of the street then I would buy him the bus ticket. We met there forty-five minutes later. I waited with him until his bus was ready to leave, before giving him £20 and leaving him to get onto the bus. I don't know whether he did or he didn't catch the bus. I didn't watch him get onto it. There has to be some trust. If he didn't get onto the bus he made a decision not to. I had given him hope and an opportunity. It was up to him to take it. He wasn't in the doorway when I walked by again.

Sometimes people need encouragement, a conversation, some reassurance and opportunity. I remember Christmas Day in 2017 when I met a man who had been sleeping close to the seafront in my home town under a tarpaulin. It was a miserable day and he had been walking the streets on his own before one of the Operation Snow volunteers had picked him up and brought him to the community venue. The first thing he needed was dry clothes. Then a quick medical check-up of his feet, which had become wet and sore. That day, he was warm, dry and ate well. He also had good company. He had nowhere to stay that night, which meant he would be sleeping on the streets again. Operation Snow arranged a travel lodge for him for a few nights and met with him daily to give him some food. He managed to get put up by a friend, which was great. I didn't hear from him for about four months and then one day, he called the business and left a message to thank us for helping him. He didn't leave a number so we couldn't return his call. It was good to know he was okay and that our support had helped him. He told me he would come back and help cook for Operation Snow when he was back on his feet because he was a trained chef. I encouraged this thought. He would be welcome.

There are so many populations and communities to help. Some have very basic needs whereas others are quite complex. Here is where remembering your roots is important again; if you do not '*own*' your stuff and are not emotionally resilient, you may turn to other ways of coping and at worst crime and problematic substance use.

I'd like to work with the aboriginal community in Australia. (I am currently staying in Australia whilst doing the final edits of the book and I have just been accepted onto the Australian nursing register to practice as a mental health nurse so I am hopeful it will happen. I'm making plans so that it can). Within this group of people there is a high rate of substance use issues, safeguarding concerns and a deficit in mental health treatment options available. I'm eager to engage with communities and groups of people who would not readily walk into treatment and people affected by these concerns are less likely to seek help. This is similar for numerous other cultures and communities worldwide.

When I set up my first company, Arterne: Enriching the next generation CIC I focused on how it could impact positively within healthcare, social care and education. I've always said that "little tug boats can pull big ships". I wanted the company to have a significant impact within communities and as a not-for-profit company all monies go back into the business for social purpose and community gain. It was important for me to ensure that help could be accessed as early as possible for any presenting problem. This had been a message I had promoted within all of my roles in larger organisations, which had been ignored in favour of reacting to situations of severity and crisis. Early intervention can start from the minute you're even being thought about. It can also mean getting in quickly to resolve any problem that is arising at any age. You need your parents and carers to understand this, explain it to you at the right time and get the help they need in order to make life different for you. This is both as a child and as an adult because that's what shapes us. Like we've already discussed, repeating patterns of behaviour exist and they can come from generations of people that you've never even met.

When Laurie went to study in New York Film Academy to pursue her dreams of becoming an actor, I had this realisation that I had changed her life chances through making specific decisions about how I wanted to bring her up. This was purposefully different to my upbringing, particularly the older she got. It's very easy to slip into generational patterns and behaviours. We sometimes do what we're expected to do because that's the way it is. I wanted Laurie to make her own decisions about the life she wanted and most of all, I wanted her to be happy and love who she is, which is an intelligent, beautiful and talented women. I'm proud of her and I make sure she knows she is loved for who she is (I can see her rolling her eyes at me now whilst she's reading this and saying, "Okay, Big C").

## L.O.V.E LEADERSHIP IN ACTION

### Situational Depression and Homelessness to Hope, by Clint Jones

"I met Cindy several years ago when she was brought in by the CEO of a children and young people's charity for which I was on the board of trustees. Cindy had been doing work with the CEO and psychologist at the time, as well as volunteering for the groups run by the charity. She was initially an advisor and then became the clinical lead for the trustee board. I no longer have a connection with that charity although I have kept contact with some of the people who were involved in it. Plymouth is quite small. It's more like a village so I already knew of Cindy through other people and had heard positive things about her. She's very positive, very distinct. That is where this L.O.V.E Leadership methodology comes from—her positive outlook on things and proactive spin she puts on anything that is happening. I got to know her as a friend and as a peer.

"My marriage broke down at the same time I was working a job I absolutely despised doing, but I couldn't just give everything up. I was never medically diagnosed but I think I was going through a nervous breakdown. I was struggling with a lot of things in my life. It was a chaotic time and at times, quite self-destructive. Not a great place to be. Everything was happening at the same time. Cindy was away in Ireland at the final straw of my marriage and I ended up homeless. I managed to find somewhere to stay, but it wasn't somewhere I could have my two boys. She messaged me, asking what happened. I briefly explained. Then when she got back from Ireland, she said, why don't you just live in my house? She and Andy had another house. This was a house I could not have been able to afford on the open market. Cindy just wanted us to be safe while I figured out my next move.

"Cindy gave me this house to live in, which was phenomenal. She gave me the space and breathing room to figure out things. It gave me a nice home environment for the kids for the transition period, as I didn't want them to sleep in a pull-out bed. I wanted them to have consistency. Cindy didn't pressure me for money. She was very supportive. She took additional time to come and see me at work and talk to me about the things I was going through, and never in a judgmental way. She also treated me with auricular acupuncture. It opened me up to the idea of talking about stuff.

"In return, I tried to help her with projects like Operation Snow, based around helping those who needed it around the Christmas period. People who were homeless, families who didn't have much and people on their own. She pulled together this project with various partners, providing support and aid. There, I met my partner who was helping out on Christmas Day. Inadvertently, Cindy was also responsible for me and Jo getting together, which was quite nice!"

## Reflection From the Heart

I set up Operation Snow to spread unconditional love and Christmas spirit after my experience of volunteering at a local church on Christmas Day the previous year. I wanted to remove barriers between groups of people and provide people with a place to go on Christmas Day, not to give something up, to spend Christmas with others who they may or may not know. I remember Clint and Jo meeting there, and I know I felt hesitant about either of them rushing into anything. This links back to 'own' in the L.O.V.E Leadership model and making sure it starts from within. I was delighted for them when I heard that a while later, they were in a relationship together. I was even more pleased when Clint proposed at Operation Snow in 2017 and Jo said, "Yes!"

# Chapter 9

## *Voice*

HAVE YOU THOUGHT ABOUT WHAT a conversation actually is? How powerful it can be? I mentioned earlier that much of my work with people is done through conversation. This includes verbal and non-verbal communications. Sometimes the conversation is more structured than at other times. It is an approach determined by the needs of the individual, team or organisation.

I recall an experience where I was working with two employees in another organisation who were in conflict with one another. I took both of them together to the garden area for forty-five minutes to help to remove the barriers within their communications and relationships. I encouraged both of these practitioners, told them how amazing I thought they were and how great it was for them to be different from one another. This was not for the first time—repeated communications about the same things are needed within some teams in order to effect change and improvements. Some of the challenge for them was that they both sought reassurance from outside of themselves, without working on feeling it first inside themselves. This had made the relationship between them tense at times as one practitioner had been unaware of the comparison she had been making about herself against the other very knowledgeable and experienced practitioner. This competitiveness had affected their entire relationship and ability to work together for the benefit of the charity and the people being supported by it. Fear of not being good enough had set in. This had affected judgements and perceptions. Their fear is that competition will supersede common sense and skill set and that they will get "thrown under the bus" by another vying for that seat. Instead of talking with one another about their fears, anxieties or frustrations, they had chosen to speak about one another to other people in the team, which was destructive within the team working. This preoccupation had impacted negatively on their performance and team spirit. They forgot about the people they were helping, which needed to be at the forefront of their mind. Formal mediation was offered to both practitioners and rejected by one of the practitioners after making a formal complaint about their colleague. This situation may have improved if they had found their voice and used it in a conversation with one another. This was not the only challenge in the team at the time. The small team had been troubled with an employee who had moved on in her role yet left a trail of unpleasant energy as she tried to discredit the more knowledgeable and experienced practitioner by speaking about him in a derogatory way. This had impacted negatively on the ability of the two colleagues I had spoken with to build a relationship, as mistrust was created between them early on in their relationship by spoken untruths from another individual. An open dialogue between them both would have helped improve the connectedness.

The L.O.V.E Leadership model promotes you to have your voice and to not be afraid to use it. There are two other things to consider here when this is said. One is to remember that if you have a voice, then so does the person you are speaking with. This means you are therefore, required to listen as well as use your voice. They compliment one another. The other consideration is having a voice needs to be influenced by good intentions and empowering interactions. Using a voice to verbally abuse or gossip about someone is not advocated within the L.O.V.E Leadership model. Having a voice does not mean that your perception of a situation or person is correct and whilst you may speak these views out loud if the intention behind this is to discredit or attack someone personally this should not be promoted by anyone in a family unit, friendship group or a business. In fact, it should be challenged by someone in the moment that it occurs because failure to do this will create a negative environment that is mistrusting and ineffective. I've seen lots of businesses fall foul to the inability to tackle this and therefore, for people to feel they have a voice. Change is effective when things feel challenging as it's the conversation about difference or new ways that alter repeating patterns of behaviour for individuals and businesses. Empowerment can be representative of change. Giving compliments is a wonderful gift and something I encourage. In the main, if your interaction is good or well-intended, that will leave people feeling good. It's more of a challenge when you are promoting a shift in thinking or behaviours. This can be related to fear. People may feel a threat to their status, have an uncertainty about their future or their autonomy, relatedness or fairness, which needs to be understood (Rock, 2008).

As a leader or manager within a company you may not always bypass judgment either. I've landed on "Judgment Day" a few times! The challenge here is lack of dialogue and ownership some people are willing to accept to make a situation feel better. I had mentioned the woman I worked with who had nicknames for everyone in the team that were offensive and derogatory. Well, let me add here that she had attended part of a psychotherapist training and was working in a mental health service, so I expected her to have a good understanding of why using names like "Slippery Shoulders," "Golden Balls," "Madam," "Pathetic" and "Spoilt Child" to describe her colleagues was wrong. She also used to tell stories about people and describe in detail what she thought their inadequacies were. Sadly, group think had occurred within the senior leadership team and her actions and conversations had gone unchallenged, until she met me. No one was safe from her toxic opinions, not even the senior leadership team. I don't know what she called me—I can only imagine that it was deeply unpleasant!

Now, what was interesting was instead of owning up to her unacceptable behaviour and discussions when it was tackled, she felt like I was bullying her and went to gain the vote of the people who she had been derogatory about for their support against how badly she was being treated by me. What happened next was ironic really. I was addressing her behaviour that was unacceptable towards a group of people, who then unknowingly supported the person who had regularly discredited each member of them. She didn't tell them why we were in conflict. She had managed to place herself in the role of 'victim' when in fact she had been 'perpetrator' who had been told by me to stop. I had sought HR support to tackle this situation as it had been allowed to go on unchallenged for many years.

I do believe in the power of voice and we see lots of examples in society where this is used for good, but I believe we cannot support ill-intentioned or disempowering voices to dominate lives or businesses. I personally don't want to work in a business that promotes a culture of gossip, bullying behaviours and a culture of fear. I don't think anyone would. So why does it happen? I hear many people talk about the system or the culture of a place. What's interesting to me is that people make up the system; it's not something unrelated to you or me. This can only mean one thing. If we want the system we work or live in to be different then we need to take the steps to make a difference and support others to do the same. Communications are important and there are many ways to improve these. I often promote "TypeCoach" based on personality type (2019) as something easy to understand and implement, which helps people to step into the shoes of someone else. I want to be a part of a business that stands for empowering each other and this is promoted within my companies. It is also promoted through my life and interactions with people. And through L.O.V.E Leadership.

## Voice May Mean You Stand Alone

I can recall many occasions in which I have been the lone voice in saying something known by others to be doing the right thing. Very rarely have others stood beside me in speaking about something contentious through fear of being disciplined, bullied, ostracised, scapegoated or simply unpopular. I have a skill in speaking openly and believe that support and challenge roles in businesses are equally important. I agree that people want to hear how well they are performing, what they are achieving or the positive progress. Simultaneously, I believe that conversation needs to be open for challenge, conflict, difference or change. And this needn't be viewed as negative or critical. Some of the best learning comes from situations that aren't going well. People would benefit from being encouraged to be the lone voice and not fear the repercussions of taking the chance (or opportunity).

I will speak very sensitively about an experience I was involved in. I had been meeting with a nurse in the UK whom I had been offering clinical supervision. This is a requirement of nursing practice and includes personal and professional development discussions with your named supervisor as well as reflection upon any work that you might be undertaking as a nurse. It was during one of these sessions I was first informed that a nurse had shaved the pubic hair of a young person whilst they were a patient in a psychiatric hospital. I was in disbelief initially and clarified what I had been told. What became apparent was that it had happened before, to others and other people working there were aware. In my opinion, to physically take a razor to shave the pubic region of a minor in your care, whether consensual of not, was beyond the realms of a nursing role unless you were preparing someone for surgery or helping them to manage an out of-control lice infestation. I sought a discussion with my line manager about the concerns I had who was just as surprised as I was about the alleged situations, and planned a safeguarding investigation. As a result of this, both my manager and I were severely bullied by individuals and senior members of the organisation's leadership structure, which never ceased. What transpired through the investigation was everyone knew it was happening and no one thought that it shouldn't happen. There were about twenty members of the team at that time. Senior team members of the hospital staff were outraged it was being questioned and they openly referred to the situation as "pube-gate". This was supported by the linked community services staff who were upset that their colleagues had been put through such an ordeal.

It became apparent that it certainly was an organisational culture and behaviour that had never been questioned or challenged. It demonstrated a clear overstepping of boundaries and limited understanding about why it could not continue to happen.

I want to talk briefly about the bullying that occurred. This had affected both me and my manager. My manager at the time was a role model to me. She had an enthusiasm and energy that drew me to work within the services that she led. I learned a lot from her and we worked well together. We became friends, too, which changed after our experiences through no fault of our own. Encouraged by my manager and a peer, I wrote to the organisation's CEO and HR lead about the bullying I was experiencing. I had already visited the CEO several times before to share my experiences of what was happening and nothing was being addressed. It took a great deal of courage to take these steps and voice what was happening to me which had arisen as a result of me telling my manager about the concerns I had heard in the clinical supervision session. I never expected to be asked by them to withdraw my letter. I was in utter disbelief. What followed this was deeply unprofessional and unpleasant for both my manager and I. I will not go into detail here about what happened: however, I will share the experience I had included, all of the named bullies being sent copies of my detailed letter about their behaviours, which they then shared with other people with no recompense. I was told I had to attend a meeting on my own with all the bullies I had listed, their managers and senior leadership team. There were more than ten people there—all with copies of my letter.

At this meeting, I was forced into a position to accept individual meetings with the bullies and their managers rather than a processed-driven investigation taking place. This is where I faced up to an hour-long interrogation each time by both the bully and their manager, telling me I had lied. This happened three times although the last meeting was cut short by fifteen minutes because I couldn't stop crying during it, so much so I could no longer speak I was then issued a manager's code of conduct by the CEO. I knew I had to get through this experience and use it to do good. Let's face it: All of this came out of me reporting a suspected safeguarding concern, which my manager agreed needed to be investigated. I remember thinking, *Was that so wrong?*

I did make it through. It has been said that I've got "balls of steel". Now I just wanted the bullying to stop happening and followed the organisational policy to try and achieve that. Sadly, that wasn't supported in the way that it could have been. The union representative I was provided with later had long-term relationships with many of the people I've spoken about and told me that "sometimes you have to forget about your principles." That was just before she retired. In my opinion, she did a good job forgetting about having principles around safeguarding and bullying. This was not something I wanted to forget. I have to say I don't agree and had I not felt so warn out by it all at the time, I may have been able to tell her what I thought, too—that she was colluding with unacceptable behaviours.

This experience taught me a great deal and helped shape who I have become. I am courageous and have integrity. L.O.V.E Leadership assisted and if I was faced with a similar situation in the future I would do it again.

To further discuss the importance of not being afraid to be a lone voice, I recall a meeting I attend at a drug and alcohol service with a senior leadership team. It was during the course of some service development I was assisting with, and we were discussing two people both accessing treatment at the same time and getting into a relationship with one another, which was frowned upon; relationships developing whilst in treatment can have a detrimental effect upon the intended goals. The discussion had concluded that "he" had to be moved from his current placement in to another placement out of the area.

I asked why we were talking about moving him on and highlighted that we needed to treat him and her as specialists in this area of work. No one agreed with me until the psychiatrist reflected and could see where I was coming from. With her support we were able to get the best outcome for both of the people in treatment rather than appear to punish someone for the very thing that keeps them stuck in a life of problematic substance use. This decision was a life-changing decision for either one of them and it was something I had to voice, provide my rationale, albeit initially alone.

## What Keeps Your Courage Up?

Most people want to do the right thing. There are things that sometimes make speaking up or being a lone voice a challenge and my role in discussing this isn't to be critical. It's to help increase understanding so that people can feel empowered to stand for what they believe in, just like I do. Being true to yourself is important. As is; Integrity. Heart. Love. Believing in people and good intentions is essential. Doing the right thing is not always easy; it is something that can be decided.

How you interpret a conversation or situation is in your control as is what you would do next. I always consider a situation based on what I would want if this were my family, friend, or colleague. I know I would want the best for them. This shows up in what I do every day; it's natural and that is how I view it. Seeing people as whole, stepping into their shoes and putting them first is possible. It takes practice.

Whether music, art, another activity, being able to express yourself in whatever way you can is important. If you can learn to express yourself, that will help your self-esteem, which will strengthen your voice.

I really didn't like my voice at one point. When I was asked to speak as a keynote at a UK national conference alongside some senior commissioners in children's health, I doubted my ability. I took singing lessons initially, which did help. I thought if I could sing in front of people, then I could talk in front of people! I asked someone to help me. She was a musician and the first time we met for singing practice, I hid under my long hair, mumbling and avoiding eye contact. I've developed since then. I've sung in so many pubs with my friend at karaoke bars, fun day events, even on the street, and not because I'm a great performer. It's because I love how it makes me feel. I love the energy. I can get up and sing a few songs because I like it. I enjoy the energetic connection between me singing and the people I am with at the time.

The thing is, I thought it was initially the sound of my voice I didn't like. It actually wasn't that. It was because I didn't like myself and I didn't think I had anything valuable to say. I remember thinking, *What do I know? Who am I? I'm nobody.* This was a lifelong view of me. This is what I had to address within me. That negative self-belief persists if you allow it to. That's what I had to work on. Once I had achieved that for myself I could be an encourager of others.

**Important: Feel the fear and do it anyway!**

That is why I packaged up the L.O.V.E Leadership model. I've achieved wonderful things, live a happy life, lead successful businesses and the L.O.V.E Leadership model has helped me do that. It is your turn to benefit from it.

## WELLNESS WARRIOR

Helen Davies, Social Worker

Helen is an experienced health and well-being strategist, manager and practitioner with a history of success at local, regional and national levels. She has worked with a diverse range of individuals of all ages, who have had additional needs such as learning disabilities, mental health issues and/or challenging behaviours. At one point, she worked her way up to the position of team manager for a supported living establishment, with 50 staff supporting 20 service users. Here, Helen offers substantial solutions for holistic care, but first, I have to ask her what it was like to manage a large staff group.

**Q: What did all this experience teach you about mental health?**

**A:** Managing took me away from the service users who I enjoyed working with, it was also an extremely stressful time and affected my home life. I found I could never switch off and due to often having on-call duties and covering staff absences I found myself exhausted and sought support from my GP. I was diagnosed with stress and depression and placed on medication. My employers recognised that I was becoming unwell and offered me a change of job role which allowed me to focus on the clinical aspect of the role. I was allowed to use my initiative and given the autonomy to develop the service users support plans. During this time, I was supervised by a clinical psychologist who challenged me and often made me feel uncomfortable and deskilled during the first few months of our working together. However, over time, I came to realise that he was beneficial to my learning and self-development. During this time, I pursued short courses in various therapeutic techniques such as person-centred counselling, Cognitive Behavioural Therapy (CBT) and Mindfulness. This led me to applying for a research position at Bangor University. Here, I worked on a feasibility project examining the effectiveness of mindfulness to reduce anger in people with learning disabilities. After a long trajectory, Social Work appealed as it seemed the natural progression from previous roles. Having worked with Social Workers as part of a Multi-Disciplinary Team it was a role I believed I could perform competently and with the experience I already have I felt I would be able to connect with individuals and essential 'help' them.

Looking back, I would not have considered Social Work as my first degree, I would have lacked the confidence. I now feel I have enough life experience to feel more confident in the prospective role of Social Worker. The level of responsibility associated with this role would have sat uncomfortably with me, and due to my own anxieties I feel I would not have coped with the course prior to this point.

**Q: What have you learned from L.O.V.E Leadership?**

**A:** I've learned more than I could have imagined. However, some key learning points are:

- **Leadership.** Although I have worked as a manager, supervising over 50 staff during one period, I never considered myself as a leader. However, I have learnt from that even if I am not leading teams I am responsible for how I lead myself. This model of leadership has encouraged me to own my stuff and voice my opinions/thoughts rather than remaining quiet. Integrity has also become important to me, questioning why things are done a particular way and questioning when it doesn't feel right.
- **Confidence.** I have been encouraged to work outside of my comfort zone. I have been supported to challenge my fears,

particularly in reference to presenting information, meeting new people, and leading groups.

- **Communication skills.** I have found myself now asking how I can support others, what they need, rather than trying to rescue them or fix their problem for them.

I now know that I possess a wealth of experience and knowledge and although I initially felt de-skilled and incompetent in my new role as a student social worker, L.O.V.E Leadership has been able to make me aware of the links between the work I am doing now and my skills and knowledge.

**Q: How have you grown since focusing your career on mental health?**

**A:** I have become more understanding and empathetic. Being able to see a person as an individual and understanding their needs holistically. Recognising that there may be a presenting problem, however there may also be a wealth of underlying issues, including larger socio-cultural issues, housing needs, financial difficulties etc.

I have become more understanding in my personal relationships, I am able to take more time to consider problems and place myself in the other person's shoes. I am less anxious in general, and more willing to try new things having realised how fortunate I am and that there is learning in all new challenges, even if I fail. I am also more knowledgeable and therefore, find myself giving more accurate advice, weighing up information, and offering different perspectives. I have also started to become more passionate about advocating for people rights- I think this has stemmed from a combination of knowledge regarding the law and a more recent and deeper understanding of social justice.

Also I have become far more reflective. This has meant that I consider things more rationally, accept situations as they are, evaluate and plan a course of action.

**Q: When it comes to mental health, what needs to change?**

**A:** I do not believe there is one single answer. It is a complex, interrelated system that requires various changes.

- Funding. Austerity has taken its toll on health and social care in England. Preventative services have been cut back meaning that issues are having to be dealt with when they reach crisis point. There is an increasing reliance on the voluntary sector to provide services.
- Homelessness. We are short of social housing, I have seen an increase on homeless people on the streets of Plymouth over the past few years. Women who I have been working with on placement often arrive homeless and can't relocate due to the lack of housing or their needs not considered enough to warrant housing.
- People attitudes. There continues to be stigma around mental health, issues are not considered in the same way as physical health issues.
- Social Care and Health services need to be more joined up. This is beginning to happen, and there is often a crossover between health and social care needs, however neither has the budget to consider all of the person's needs.
- The culture of Western Society. We are often individualistic, always wanting more. I have over the past few years practiced Mindfulness. I find that being present, in the moment, can often refocus me. It is a fine balancing act between issues in the here and now being addressed and what can be achieved form discussing the past and future.

A lot could be achieved by people being kind. Saying hello to their neighbours and looking out for one another. L.O.V.E Leadership has a lot to offer. I believed these qualities were something that came with age, though discussion made me realise that it was actually experience and knowledge. I may have developed these skills sooner had I had someone impress this information on me sooner.

I've explored what theory or technique to use with individuals when they are at crisis. First, you must genuinely care, which helps people open up. I feel that those suffering with mental illness are often misunderstood, judged and feared. However, Maslow's Hierarchy of Needs applies to them just as it does everyone else. Instilling hope in others is particularly powerful for change behaviours.

# Chapter 10

## *Empower*

I LIKE TO CELEBRATE PEOPLE FOR who they are. I look at people's qualities and see their goodness. I want to understand them. If someone comes in and shouts at me, I want to understand where they are in that moment mentally. Do I remind them of someone? It is because they feel like they've never had their voice heard? Do they have a problem with their hearing? If I start to get bitter without trying to realise what's going on, I will only breathe more negativity on the situation.

I freelanced at a hair and beauty salon, providing auricular acupuncture. Again, I appreciate complementary approaches as well as the medical modalities. The hair dresser had been in an abusive relationship with a man that had a lot of money. She had three children with him. I knew her after she left him for good. He still had the three children. These children wouldn't have anything to do with her because their father had turned them against her. He told them she had an affair on him and left. That's not exactly what happened. She was a broken woman. I would get my hair done there and we would talk extensively.

One of the hazards of my job is that whatever I do, where ever I go, someone will confide in me about an intense situation. I could be on a night out, standing on a sidewalk waiting for a taxi, eating chips on the street, or having my hair done. I will always listen. I don't mind. I always talked to her about having hope. I treated her with auricular acupuncture and listened. I helped her as a mental health nurse, I suppose. All those skills don't just sit there and do nothing. It's the whole of you that supports others.

I tried to give her hope and kept repeating, "One day..." She didn't believe it. She tolerated those words regarding her children. Then she messaged me not so long ago. I was so blown away by it. One of her sons returned to live with her. Lots happened in between that. Mother's Day, she posted something on social media. It made me smile so big. She talked about me saving her and giving her hope. She had not wanted her life any longer, but I made her want to carry on. I didn't realise how much it meant to her. Then the penny dropped when I read the news about her reuniting with her son.

## L.O.V.E LEADERSHIP IN ACTION

Despair to Miracles, by Anonymous

"Cindy and her teachings came at a pivotal point in my life. I was living at rock bottom even though I had gotten a new job, a new house.

"When I broke up with my husband, I had three children, and it was a really bad breakup. None of my boys had seen or spoken to me in over ten years. In the last year, I have one of them living with me. I don't want to ever jeopardise getting the other two back. So, when I met Cindy, I had a new house, new job, and I started working in a village. I was finding it really difficult to cope. I could not concede with my husband and the boys were 11, 12 and 13 so we were quite influenced by him. I thought my children would come back with me. But he has money and influence.

"I just spiralled. I found a new job and tried to focus on work despite all the problems. I couldn't stop crying."

"Cindy came in one day and asked, 'Are you okay?' That was the worst question anyone could ask me at the time because you want to be treated normally.

"She asked, 'Do you need help?' I agreed and went upstairs with her. She said, "I know you're not seeing your boys and you're heartbroken. You're trying to get yourself together and you're not coping."

"I said, 'No, I'm not. Every time I see children, I look at them and wonder, what are mine doing today? Where are they? I can't seem to get past it. I'm a mum and those are my children!"

"Cindy recommended auricular acupuncture in order to relieve some pressure. I was like, really? How does this work? Will that stop me from crying? She said, it will help regulate your emotions and reduce stress. I hate needles, so when she put them in my ears I thought, oh no! Then believe it or not, after a few sessions, I stopped crying. She was so nice to talk to and she didn't judge. She said the best thing I could do was learn to accept things and that I had done all I could at the time. It helped hearing that and afterwards I kept myself really busy. I got my confidence back and realised there was nothing wrong with me; it was the person I was with who tried to squash me down so far that I basically felt worthless.

"Just having Cindy talking to me and being the way she is, I got myself through it. It took a long time. The lesson is, don't give up."

"I had been with my husband a long time, and the boys originally lived with me for five years when we first broke up. My husband was very influential and could buy them anything. He ruined anything I did for them. After five years, I ended up going back with him because he had a girlfriend who wasn't very nice to my children. I couldn't get over what he had done to me. The feelings had all gone. He had done too much damage. He assaulted me. He was twenty years older than me. He was looking for a younger model of me. I got out before I would have gotten dumped anyway. He's still angry and can't be nice to me in any way, shape or form.

"He was very controlling. He always had what he wanted. You don't cross him. He had a business partner and they did everything together. If we had holiday, he would have to bring business partner. There's more to life than business. Before we had children, he had two children with other women. He's one of these people who will never accept responsibility for a problem, it will always be someone else's fault. I got one of my sons back but it took such a long time. He had seen how his dad behaved and realised it wasn't all my fault. I wanted to know about my son, what he's achieving, what his life was like. Then he started talking about things. He wanted to see more. He made contact. I didn't mention his dad. Then one day, I finally asked why he didn't want to see me. He said, it's because of my dad. He would say terrible things. So I would say the youngest one is more like me. My oldest one was very angry and sometimes behaved similarly to his father. You have to be realistic about your kids being individuals. You can't push yourself on someone who doesn't want the influence".

"When my youngest son came to live with me, his dad wouldn't speak to him for months. Now his dad is speaking to him and he sees his brothers. I got remarried to a man who is really lovely. He has four children. I've known hardship. I know your coping skills, good or bad, can be developed when you're a child. My twin sister died at six and three quarters. It was really difficult for my family. They couldn't hold it together. I'm lucky because my mum and dad are really nice people, but eventually they met other suitable people. There is no nastiness between them though. They still see each other and chat. You can have a normal family to a certain degree and it makes you more compassionate for other people. Having children makes you compromise in lots of ways—your schedule, career, yourself in many ways, but it needs to be like that because they need looking after. That's part of how you grow up. Having brothers and sisters help to shape who you are toward others too.

"I'm happily married today. He's not a womaniser. He's honest. He's a good family man. He's hardworking, all the things my ex-husband was not. Nice, down to earth. Good with people. My ex was wealthy, devious, a poser, probably a crook, but very charming.

"Cindy's right: everyone needs someone to listen and not judge. You also have to realise not everything is perfect in life. It's not rehearsal. This is it. All we have is now. You have to find something meaningful, even if it's about all about helping someone else. It's not just about yourself."

## Reflection From the Heart

When you're in this type of situation, whether you're male or female, you feel alone when those things are happening and you choose not to talk about it. It's hard to find someone you can trust and speak confidentially to. Sometimes it can help people to disclose aspects of your life—it lets them know that you're human and so are they. I've talked to you about my ex-husband and the challenges I had. I didn't talk to anyone about it at the time it was transpiring. I would encourage anyone going through some challenges not to wait before they speak up about it.

With the story shared by the anonymous person, it was clear she believed the situation with her children would continue that way forever. She lacked hope she would ever see them again. I saw her when she had no hope. She had hit rock bottom. She described how she felt they had been turned against her although she knew she hadn't done anything wrong. As a mother, she found that so much of a challenge because she had an ex-husband who was controlling and violent at times. He was wealthy so he could spoil the children with gifts and holidays, which she couldn't do. He was a well-known business man in the city, which was something which she feared because of his connections. In fact, I would go as far to say that she is absolutely petrified of him because of his influence and position in society. She described his controlling behaviour and how her mental health has been shaped by her experiences with him. Sometimes she thinks his abuse is still possible even though she has remarried and he's in another relationship. This is something people who have been abused do fear until they work through it.

My ex-husband has moved on to form another relationship with another person. This experience strips you of self-worth and you think you won't be listened to once you flee this type of abuse. Isolation sets in pretty quickly. Being an adult means *you should know better*—the reality is that it doesn't! Sometimes you know what is right and wrong for you, but you just can't make the change they need to make. This goes for even the strongest people. It's easy to get stuck in a rut.

That's why you need people to help and empower you to do something different. Engaging and educating people is so important in empowering people so that they can evolve.

It's true that even the smallest of interactions can have a significant impact without you even realising it. I met a fabulous woman in the last two years whilst she was freelancing in a charity I was linked with. More recently she bumped into my husband when he was playing golf and during their chat, let him know that she was training to be a nurse because of me. I had no idea that I had influenced her in this way although I do recall some fantastic discussions with her. What's important here was I had motivated her decision and empowered her to take action without even being aware. I remember we had met for a coffee one day and we were talking about her experiences related to the death of her daughter. I was quick to encourage her to follow her dreams when she told me that she thought she wanted to go back into education. She was training to become a registered mental health nurse and had told my husband "It was your wife, that's why I'm doing this." I didn't realise the significance of our time together. In fact, I just think that every interaction with someone is significant.

# Chapter 11

## *Draw Your Heart Around It*

L.O.V.E Leadership focuses on promoting how you conduct yourself as a leader of you. If you can lead yourself in a way that promotes integrity and a happy, healthy lifestyle then you can lead other things, whether that be an event, project, team, service or organisation. **L.O.V.E Leadership encourages this through: actively listening; owning your own stuff and remembering your roots; having a voice and not being afraid to use it; accepting that this is true for others; and empowerment—engaging, educating to evolve to reach self-actualisation and your desired goals.** Spreading unconditional love is equally important. Once you can understand the conscious and unconscious version of you, it's easier to make decisions and act out the behaviours that will impact positively on your life.

When you learn to empower yourself you can empower others. The intentions behind conversations and actions towards others is critical. Knowing yourself, who you're being in any given moment and coming from a good place is essential personally and professionally. The way you speak about others or a situation will affect relationships and outcomes.

L.O.V.E Leadership promotes the notion if you can achieve this for yourself then you are in a stronger position to help other people do the same. For example, if you can feel confident in who you are or your abilities, reduce negative self-talk or internal dialogue and promote a positive perception you will live a fulfilling life personally and provisionally. If you judge or talk about someone else in a derogatory way to others then this will shape your experience and perception of that person and your experience. If you interpret things with a negative lens, this is the experience that will come back to you. If your intentions are not pure or well-intended then no good can come of this for anyone. You can't blame the world on your deficiencies. You are the master of your own destiny.

Reflection on one's own actions and how it impacts upon on a situation is important and takes practice. What you do to resolve a situation you feel is not beneficial to you is in your control. Approaching things with understanding, love and integrity will promote good outcomes. Open and honest dialogue will make sure that there is a level of transparency and trust. For example, if you choose to speak about senior leaders or managers in a derogatory way, it is likely that this will be your story for any given situation where you feel challenged.

Who you show up as will impact upon you. Likewise, if you are an observer or witness to someone else speaking in this way you can choose to join in, ignore it, which promotes a view of acceptance, or you can challenge it. Understanding that people are not just defined by their job roles, and knowing they have tasks to complete within their job roles, helps to build relationships. This will help to promote good working environments and improve workplace culture.

L.O.V.E Leadership can support individual and company development through adopting its approach, alongside unconditional love for people and what you are doing. The first step is to achieve this as an individual and then help to support others to do the same. This doesn't mean that there will not be challenging conversations or situations to overcome. Life is full of ups and downs. Support and challenge is essential to develop fully. Depersonalising difference or disagreements to embrace them is beneficial. Being unwilling to let our experiences shape us fully and being open to how we can use the experiences for a positive impact helps improve life quality. Striving to be the best version of you and supporting others in this journey, too, will lead you to happiness and a life that you want to live. It will also impact positively within companies and upon business productivity. If you wake up happy, truly living the life you want, this will shine from you. Celebrating achievements and learning from unpleasant experiences is all part of the stories we have as human beings—as is supporting others to achieve their desires and full potential. #educatinghearts

# References

Almasy, Steve. "Kate Spade's husband said she battled demons but death was complete shock." CNN.com. June 7, 2018. https://www.cnn.com/2018/06/06/us/kate-spade-husband-statement/index.html.

Arterne. http://www.arterne.com.

BBC. "US school shootings: Lullabies used to teach drills." June 8, 2018. https://www.bbc.com/news/world-us-canada-44411208.

Beach Schools South West. https://www.beachschoolssouthwest.co.uk.

Beaumont-Thomas, Ben. "Coroner Confirms Cause of Linkin Park Singer Chester Bennington's Death." *The Guardian.* July 21, 2018. https://www.theguardian.com/music/2017/jul/21/linkin-park-singer-chester-bennington-hanging-coroner-confirms.

Brady, MacKenty Susan. *Mastering Your Inner Critic...and 7 Other High Hurdles to Advancement.* McGraw-Hill Professional, New York. December 3, 2018.

Breiding, Matthew J. et al. "Prevalence and Characteristics of Sexual Violence, Stalking, and Intimate Partner Violence Victimization – National Intimate Partner and Sexual Violence Survey, United States, 2011." *Centers for Disease Control and Prevention Morbidity and Mortality Weekly Report.* Vol. 63, No. 8 (2014): 7.

Curcio, J. "Carl Jung: In Critique and Defense." *Modern Mythology*. December 3, 2015. https://modernmythology.net/carl-jung-in-critique-and-defense-6e098065bf98.

Ehmke, Rachel. "How Using Social Media Affects Teenagers." Child Mind Institute. https://childmind.org/article/how-using-social-media-affects-teenagers/.

Heller, Corinne. "Inside Anthony Bourdain's Final Days Before His Death." *E! News.* June 9, 2018. https://www.eonline.com/news/942826/inside-anthony-bourdain-s-final-days-before-his-death.

Herbst, Diane. "Kevin Hines Survived a Jump Off the Golden Gate Bridge. Now, He's Helping Others Avoid Suicide." PSYCOM. https://www.psycom.net/kevin-hines-survived-golden-gate-bridge-suicide/.

Hodgkin, K. *Madness in Seventeenth-Century Autobiography.* New York: Palgrave Macmillan. 2007.

Historic England. "The growth of the asylum, a parallel world."https://historicengland.org.uk/research/inclusive-heritage/disability-history/1832-1914/the-growth-of-the-asylum

LaVito, Angelica. "Anxiety is expensive: Employee mental health costs rise twice as fast as all other medical expenses." *CNBC.* September 27, 2018. https://www.cnbc.com/2018/09/26/employers-are-starting-to-think-about-healthy-differently.html.

Luft, Joseph, and Harry Ingham. The Johari Window Model. 1955.

Markel, Howard. "Marilyn Monroe and the Prescription Drugs That Killed Her." *PBS.org.* August 5, 2016. *https://www.pbs.org/newshour/health/marilyn-monroe-and-the-prescription-drugs-that-killed-her.*

Mental Health Foundation. "Added Value: Mental health as a workplace asset." Mental Health Foundation: London. 2016.

Mental Health Interventions and Services for Vulnerable Children and Young People. London: Jessica Kingsley. P. 50-80.

Newport Academy. "Britain's Royal Family Tackles Mental Health Stigma." May 18, 2018. https://www.newportacademy.com/resources/mental-health/royal-family/.

Nicholls, Camilla. "Employers Must Do More to Protect the Mental Health of Staff." *The Guardian.* November 12, 2018. https://www.theguardian.com/commentisfree/2018/nov/12/employers-do-more-protect-mental-health-staff.

Morgan, Nicola. *Blame My Brain.* London: Walker. 1994

National Institute of Mental Health. "Men and Mental Health." 2016. https://www.nimh.nih.gov/health/topics/men-and-mental-health/index.shtml.

Office of National Statistics. Crime Survey for England and Wales. 2016._____."Suicide by Occupation, England: 2011-2015: Analysis of deaths from suicide in different occupational groups for people aged 20-64 years, based on deaths registered in England between 2011 and 2015." Published in partnership with David Gunnell, Professor of Epidemiology, University of Bristol.

Onyett, Steve. "Leadership for Change in Mental Health Services," *Mental Health Review Journal*, Vol. 7 Issue: 4, pp.20-23, 2007. https://doi.org/10.1108/13619322200200036.

Reade, Brian. "Gary Speed's Widow Speaks of His Suicide and Reveals Torment from Age 17." *Mirror.* November

27, 2018. https://www.mirror.co.uk/sport/football/news/gary-speeds-widow-speaks-suicide-13256742.

Rock, David. "SCARF: a brain-based model for collaborating with and influencing others." *NeuroLeadership Journal.* Issue 1, 2008. pp. 1-9.

Samaritans. "Suicide Statistics Report: Latest statistics for the UK and Republic of Ireland." December 2018.

Siegler, Kirk. "How One Colorado Town is Tackling Suicide Prevention—Starting with the Kids." NPR. October 23, 2018. https://www.npr.org/sections/health-shots/2018/10/23/658834805/how-one-colorado-town-is-tackling-suicide-prevention-starting-with-the-kids.

STORM. https://stormskillstraining.com.

Sugar Smart UK. https://www.sugarsmartuk.org.

Telling, Gillian. "Inside Kurt Cobain's Tragic Suicide 24 Years After the Nirvana Legend's Death." *People.* April 5, 2018. https://people.com/music/kurt-cobain-inside-suicide-death-anniversary/.

TypeCoach. https://type-coach.com/types.

U.S Department of Health and Human Services. "Morbidity and Mortality

Weekly Report: Suicide Rates by Major Occupational Group- 17 States, 2012 and 2015." Vol 67, No 45, P.1253-1260.

Warner-Gale, F. "Children's and parents'/carers' perceptions of mentalhealth and stigma." Unpublished PhD thesis: University of Leicester. 2006. _____. "Tackling the stigma of mental health in vulnerable children and young people." National CAMHS Support Services. 2011.

World Health Organization. "Investing in Mental Health Yearly Report. Department of Mental Health and Substance Dependence, Noncommunicable Diseases and Mental Health. 2019._____. "Suicide Data." https://www.who.int/mental_health/prevention/suicide/suicideprevent/en/.

Wilson, Andrew. "The Final Days of Alexander McQueen." *Newsweek.* July 6, 2015. https://www.newsweek.com/final-days-alexander-mcqueen-357262.

Youn, Soo. "Robin Williams: Autopsy Confirms Death by Suicide." *The Hollywood Reporter.* November 7, 2014https://www.hollywoodreporter.com/news/robin-williams-autopsy-confirms-death-746194.

# About the Author

AFTER STARTING HER TRAINING IN Plymouth, 1997, Cindy Willcocks qualified as a Registered Mental Health Nurse (RMHN) in February 2000. Since completing her initial training, Cindy has studied extensively to enhance her skill set in order to serve various populations.

In the final year of training, Cindy was based at HMP Dartmoor working to support the visiting Consultant Psychiatrist and detainees. It was her work at HMP Dartmoor that sparked her interest in studying Auricular Acupuncture, which she has now practiced for over 18 years, leading to her role as South West Regional Assessor of other practitioners on behalf of The College of Auricular Acupuncture.

Cindy has worked across a number of sectors focusing on education, health and social care, in a variety of community and inpatient settings, specialising in mental health and substance use across all ages. Most importantly, Cindy has always been a strong advocate for the people using the services she has worked within and has empowered individuals, children, young people and their families to have a 'voice' in service developments at all levels.

Working to effect change within whole systems was a development that Cindy welcomed as an extension of her clinical work. Cindy has been successful in various change management roles, championing the reduction of stigma attached to the mental health term. She has received national recognition for her passionate public advocacy.

Cindy has also volunteered for local charitable causes and boards, acting as a trustee for The National Association for Primary Mental Health Work and CAMHS Training, Jeremiah's Journey, Lifeworks, Plymouth Octopus Project.

Promoting the message of "no health without mental health" focused on spreading unconditional love. Cindy has continued her work by founding Arterne: Enriching, the next generation CIC and Arterne 2 Nurse Limited. The creation of 'L.O.V.E Leadership' is captured in her book, *Draw A Heart Around It: A Revolutionary Mental Heath Treatment for Individuals and Companies.*

Lightning Source UK Ltd.
Milton Keynes UK
UKHW041850130720
366477UK00001B/6